LAWS AND LEGISLATION

RECESS APPOINTMENT POWER

IMPLICATIONS AND ANALYSES OF *NOEL CANNING V. NLRB*

LAWS AND LEGISLATION

Additional books in this series can be found on Nova's website under the Series tab.

Additional E-books in this series can be found on Nova's website under the E-book tab.

LAWS AND LEGISLATION

RECESS APPOINTMENT POWER

IMPLICATIONS AND ANALYSES OF *NOEL CANNING V. NLRB*

CHASE N. MORRISON
EDITOR

New York

For permission to use material from this book please contact us:
Telephone 631-231-7269; Fax 631-231-8175
Web Site: http://www.novapublishers.com

Library of Congress Cataloging-in-Publication Data

ISBN: 978-1-62948-675-8

Published by Nova Science Publishers, Inc. † New York

CONTENTS

PREFACE

This book begins with a general legal overview of the Recess Appointments Clause and a discussion of applicable case law that existed prior to the D.C. Circuit's decision in Noel Canning. In Noel Canning v. National Labor Relations Board, the U.S. Court of Appeals for the District of Columbia Circuit (D.C. Circuit) ruled that President Obama's appointments of three Members to the National Labor Relations Board (NLRB) were constitutionally invalid. This book focuses on the ramifications that the Noel Canning decision might have on the President's authority to make recess appointment by providing a legal analysis of Noel Canning and the applicable case law that existed prior to that decision. The U.S. Constitution explicitly provides the President with two methods of appointing officers of the United States. This book also provides an overview of the Recess Appointments Clause, exploring its historical application and legal interpretation by the executive branch, the courts, and the Comptroller General. It also reflects on the U.S. Court of Appeals for the D.C. Circuit's decision in Noel Canning v. Nat'l Labor Relations Board, which held that the President's three recess appointments to the National Labor Relations Board (NLRB) were invalid.

Chapter 1 – Under the Appointments Clause, the President is empowered to nominate and appoint principal officers of the United States, but only with the advice and consent of the Senate. In addition to this general appointment authority, the Recess Appointments Clause permits the President to make temporary appointments, without Senate approval, during periods in which the Senate is not in session. On January 4, 2012, while the Senate was holding periodic "pro forma" sessions, President Obama invoked his recess appointment power and unilaterally appointed Richard Cordray as Director of the Consumer Financial Protection Bureau (CFPB) and Terrence F. Flynn,

Sharon Block, and Richard F. Griffin Jr. as Members of the National Labor Relations Board (NLRB).

The President's recess appointments were ultimately challenged by parties affected by actions taken by the appointed officials, and on January 25, 2013, the U.S. Court of Appeals for the District of Columbia Circuit (D.C. Circuit) became the first court to evaluate the merits of the President's appointments. In a broad decision entitled *Noel Canning v. National Labor Relations Board*, the court invalidated the appointment of all three NLRB Board Members. In reaching its decision, the D.C. Circuit concluded that under the Recess Appointments Clause, the President may only make recess appointments during a formal intersession recess (a recess between the end of one session of Congress and the start of another), *and* only to fill those vacancies that arose during the intersession recess in which the appointment was made.

Although the D.C. Circuit's actual order in *Noel Canning* directly applies only to the NLRB's authority to undertake the single action at issue in the case, the court's interpretation of the President's recess appointment authority could have a substantial impact on the future division of power between the President and Congress in the filling of vacancies. If affirmed by the Supreme Court, the likely effect of the reasoning adopted in *Noel Canning* would be a shift toward increased Senate control over the appointment of government officials and a decrease in the frequency of presidential recess appointments.

This report begins with a general legal overview of the Recess Appointments Clause and a discussion of applicable case law that existed prior to the D.C. Circuit's decision in *Noel Canning*. The report then analyzes the *Noel Canning* opinion and evaluates the impact the case could have on the roles of the President and Congress in the appointments context. A companion CRS report, *Practical Implications of* Noel Canning *on the NLRB and CFPB*, provides a detailed discussion of the impact the *Noel Canning* decision may have on the functioning of the NLRB and the CFPB.

Chapter 2 – In *Noel Canning v. National Labor Relations Board*, the U.S. Court of Appeals for the District of Columbia Circuit (D.C. Circuit) ruled that President Obama's appointments of three Members to the National Labor Relations Board (NLRB) were constitutionally invalid. In reaching its decision, the D.C. Circuit concluded that under the Recess Appointments Clause, the President may only make recess appointments during a formal intersession recess (a recess between the end of one session of Congress and the start of another), *and* only to fill those vacancies that arose during the intersession recess in which the appointment was made.

The legal reasoning of the case, if adopted by other courts or affirmed by the Supreme Court, could significantly alter the relationship between the President and the Congress in the appointments context. It also would cast serious doubt upon an array of previous actions by the NLRB and its ability to function in the future. Furthermore, because Richard Cordray was appointed as Director of the Bureau of Consumer Financial Protection (CFPB) at the same time and in the same manner as the NLRB appointees, *Noel Canning* raises questions about the validity of Cordray's appointment; the validity of various actions already undertaken by the CFPB; and the authority of the CFPB to function going forward.

However, the opinion's immediate impact on the functioning of the Board may be limited because the D.C. Circuit's order in *Noel Canning* vacated only the Board's administrative ruling that the company had engaged in an unfair labor practice. The decision did not invalidate any other Board actions, nor did the court issue an injunction preventing Board Members from taking any specific actions in the future. Moreover, the decision only carries precedential value within the D.C. Circuit and in no way binds other federal courts outside of the circuit.

This report assesses the potential legal impact *Noel Canning* may have on the past and future operations of the NLRB and the CFPB.

A companion report, *The Recess Appointment Power After Noel Canning v. NLRB: Constitutional Implications*, by Todd Garvey and David H. Carpenter focuses on the ramifications that the *Noel Canning* decision might have on the President's authority to make recess appointment by providing a legal analysis of *Noel Canning* and the applicable case law that existed prior that decision. While sharing the general overview of the facts and legal reasoning necessary for understanding how *Noel Canning* might affect the NLRB and CFPB, this report does not duplicate the companion report's detailed constitutional analysis of the Recess Appointments Clause.

Chapter 3 – The U.S. Constitution explicitly provides the President with two methods of appointing officers of the United States. First, the Appointments Clause provides the President with the authority to make appointments with the advice and consent of the Senate. Specifically, Article II, Section 2, clause 2 states that the President "shall nominate, and by and with the Advice and Consent of the Senate, shall appoint Ambassadors, other public Ministers and Consuls, Judges of the supreme Court, and all other Officers of the United States, whose Appointments are not herein otherwise provided for, and which shall be established by law." Second, the Recess Appointments Clause authorizes the President to make temporary appointments unilaterally during periods when the Senate is not in session. Article II, Section 2, clause 3 provides: "The President shall have Power to fill up all Vacancies that may happen during the Recess of the Senate, by granting Commissions which shall expire at the End of their next Session."

While the Recess Appointments Clause enables the continuity of government operations, Presidents, on occasion, have exercised authority under the Clause for tactical or political purposes, appointing officials who might otherwise have difficulty securing Senate confirmation. The Recess Appointments Clause is not without its ambiguities, and the President's use of this power in light of these ambiguities has given rise to significant political and legal controversy since the beginning of the republic.

This report provides an overview of the Recess Appointments Clause, exploring its historical application and legal interpretation by the executive branch, the courts, and the Comptroller General. It also reflects the U.S. Court of Appeals for the D.C. Circuit's decision in *Noel Canning v. Nat'l Labor Relations Board*, which held that the President's three recess appointments to the National Labor Relations Board (NLRB) on January 4, 2012, were invalid. Furthermore, congressional legislation designed to prevent the President's overuse or misuse of the Clause is also explored.

In: Recess Appointment Power
Editor: Chase N. Morrison
ISBN: 978-1-62948-675-8

Chapter 1

THE RECESS APPOINTMENT POWER AFTER *NOEL CANNING V. NLRB*: CONSTITUTIONAL IMPLICATIONS*

Todd Garvey and David H. Carpenter

SUMMARY

Under the Appointments Clause, the President is empowered to nominate and appoint principal officers of the United States, but only with the advice and consent of the Senate. In addition to this general appointment authority, the Recess Appointments Clause permits the President to make temporary appointments, without Senate approval, during periods in which the Senate is not in session. On January 4, 2012, while the Senate was holding periodic "pro forma" sessions, President Obama invoked his recess appointment power and unilaterally appointed Richard Cordray as Director of the Consumer Financial Protection Bureau (CFPB) and Terrence F. Flynn, Sharon Block, and Richard F. Griffin Jr. as Members of the National Labor Relations Board (NLRB).

The President's recess appointments were ultimately challenged by parties affected by actions taken by the appointed officials, and on January 25, 2013, the U.S. Court of Appeals for the District of Columbia Circuit (D.C. Circuit) became the first court to evaluate the merits of the President's appointments.

* This is an edited, reformatted and augmented version of a Congressional Research Service publication, CRS Report for Congress R43030, dated March 27, 2013.

In a broad decision entitled *Noel Canning v. National Labor Relations Board*, the court invalidated the appointment of all three NLRB Board Members. In reaching its decision, the D.C. Circuit concluded that under the Recess Appointments Clause, the President may only make recess appointments during a formal intersession recess (a recess between the end of one session of Congress and the start of another), *and* only to fill those vacancies that arose during the intersession recess in which the appointment was made.

Although the D.C. Circuit's actual order in *Noel Canning* directly applies only to the NLRB's authority to undertake the single action at issue in the case, the court's interpretation of the President's recess appointment authority could have a substantial impact on the future division of power between the President and Congress in the filling of vacancies. If affirmed by the Supreme Court, the likely effect of the reasoning adopted in *Noel Canning* would be a shift toward increased Senate control over the appointment of government officials and a decrease in the frequency of presidential recess appointments.

This report begins with a general legal overview of the Recess Appointments Clause and a discussion of applicable case law that existed prior to the D.C. Circuit's decision in *Noel Canning*. The report then analyzes the *Noel Canning* opinion and evaluates the impact the case could have on the roles of the President and Congress in the appointments context. A companion CRS report, *Practical Implications of* Noel Canning *on the NLRB and CFPB*, provides a detailed discussion of the impact the *Noel Canning* decision may have on the functioning of the NLRB and the CFPB.

INTRODUCTION

The U.S. Constitution allocates specific roles to both the President and the Senate in the appointment of government officials. Under the Appointments Clause, the President is empowered to nominate and appoint principal officers of the United States, but only with the advice and consent of the Senate.[1] In addition to this general appointment authority, the Recess Appointments Clause permits the President to make temporary appointments, without Senate approval, during periods in which the Senate is not in session.[2] This constitutionally established appointment process, whether executed pursuant to the Appointments Clause or the Recess Appointments Clause, has often served as a source of political conflict between the President and Congress.[3] This tension between the branches is perhaps most acute when the Senate perceives the President as circumventing the Senate's constitutional "Advice and

Consent" role by unilaterally appointing officials pursuant to the Recess Appointment Clause, or, conversely, when the President perceives the Senate as obstructing his appointment power by refusing to confirm nominees the President feels are qualified.

The unique facts underlying President Obama's recess appointments of Richard Cordray as Director of the Consumer Financial Protection Bureau (CFPB) and Terrence F. Flynn, Sharon Block, and Richard F. Griffin Jr. as Members of the National Labor Relations Board (NLRB, or Board) have brought the inherent tensions of the appointments process into stark focus. Although the President had formally nominated all four officials for confirmation by the Senate during the first session of the 112th Congress, the Senate—as is its prerogative—did not confirm the President's nominees. After adjourning on December 17, 2011, the Senate agreed to hold a series of "pro forma" sessions to occur periodically until January 23, 2012.[4] Citing Senate inaction, asserting that the Senate was in recess despite the pro forma sessions, and stressing the need for a fully functioning CFPB and NLRB, on January 4, 2012, the President exercised his recess appointment power and announced the appointment of all four officials.[5]

The President's recess appointments were challenged through various lawsuits filed by parties affected by actions taken by either the CFPB or the NLRB.[6] The plaintiffs generally argued that because Cordray, Flynn, Block, and Griffin Jr. were not validly appointed, neither the CFPB nor the NLRB had authority to act. On January 25, 2013, the U.S. Court of Appeals for the District of Columbia Circuit (D.C. Circuit) became the first court to evaluate the merits of these challenges. In a case entitled *Noel Canning v. National Labor Relations Board*, the circuit court issued a broad decision invalidating the appointment of all three NLRB Board Members.[7] The court concluded that under the Recess Appointments Clause, the President may make recess appointments only during a formal intersession recess (a recess between the end of one session of Congress and the start of another), *and* only to fill those vacancies that arose during the intersession recess in which the appointment was made.[8] Although the decision directly applies only to the NLRB's authority to undertake the single action at issue in the case, the legal reasoning, if adopted by other courts or affirmed by the Supreme Court, would cast serious doubt not only upon an array of previous actions by the Board and its ability to function in the future, but also upon the validity of the President's appointment of Director Cordray; the validity of various actions already undertaken by the CFPB; and the authority of the CFPB to function going forward.[9]

This report begins with a general legal overview of the Recess Appointments Clause and a discussion of applicable case law that existed prior to the D.C. Circuit's decision in *Noel Canning*. The report then analyzes the *Noel Canning* opinion and evaluates the impact the case could have on the roles of the President and Congress in the appointments context.

THE RECESS APPOINTMENTS CLAUSE

The Constitution establishes two methods by which the President may make appointments. The Appointments Clause, which establishes the principal method of appointment, requires that the President "shall nominate, and by and with the Advice and Consent of the Senate, shall appoint Ambassadors, other public Ministers and Consuls, Judges of the supreme Court, and all other Officers of the United States whose Appointments are not herein otherwise provided for, and which shall be established by Law ..."[10]

Thus, while the Appointments Clause authorizes the President to nominate principal officers of the United States, a nominee cannot assume the powers of the office for which she has been nominated until confirmed by the Senate.[11] In addition to this general provision, the Constitution also provides an alternative method of appointment that may be exercised only "during the Recess of the Senate." The Recess Appointments Clause (Clause) establishes that "The President shall have Power to fill up all Vacancies that may happen during the Recess of the Senate, by granting Commissions which shall expire at the End of their next Session."[12]

The formative constitutional period provides only limited evidence of the intended meaning of the Clause.[13] In arguing for the Constitution's ratification by the states, however, Alexander Hamilton broadly characterized the Clause as a complement to the general appointment power that would allow the President to make temporary appointments during a Senate recess, without Senate confirmation, to offices that needed to be filled without delay.[14] Hamilton articulated the purpose of the Clause in Federalist 67, stating that the Clause was

> nothing more than a supplement to the [Appointments Clause], for the purpose of establishing an auxiliary method of appointment, in cases to which the general method was inadequate. The ordinary power of appointment is confided to the President and Senate *jointly*, and can therefore only be exercised during the session of the Senate; but as it

> would have been improper to oblige this body to be continually in session for the appointment of officers, and as vacancies might happen *in their recess*, which it might be necessary for the public service to fill without delay, the succeeding clause is evidently intended to authorize the President, *singly*, to make temporary appointments, "during the recess of the Senate, by granting commissions which shall expire at the end of their next session."[15]

Although the precise contours of the Recess Appointments Clause remain unclear, a consensus appears to have developed with respect to certain principles. For example, the Clause does not establish a lesser form of appointment. Courts that have considered the question have noted that, as a constitutional matter, a recess appointee possesses the same legal authority as a Senate confirmed appointee. Article II "neither distinguishes nor limits the powers that a recess appointee may exercise while in office."[16] As such it is widely accepted that during his term, a recess appointee "is afforded the full extent of authority commensurate with that office."[17]

It is also generally understood that, pursuant to the express terms of the Clause, the commission of a recess appointee expires at the conclusion of the Senate's "next Session" following the appointment.[18] Therefore, the point at which an individual is appointed may determine how long the officer serves. If an officer receives a recess appointment during either the first session of a Congress, or the period between the first and second sessions, the officer would serve until the end of the second session of that Congress. If an officer is appointed during the second session of a Congress, she would serve until the end of the first session of the next Congress.

Absent these few generally established principles, the Recess Appointments Clause is typically characterized as containing a number of inherent ambiguities. Most prominent among these lingering questions is the proper interpretation of the two phrases that form the very foundation of the Clause: "Vacancies that may happen during" and "the Recess of the Senate." With respect to the former phrase, must the vacancy *arise* during the recess in which the President exercises his appointment authority, or is it sufficient that the vacancy merely *exist* at the time the Senate is in recess and the appointment made? Regarding the latter, what is meant by "the Recess"? Specifically, is the President's recess appointment authority triggered only during intersession recesses (recesses *between* sessions of Congress) or may he also exercise his authority during intrasession recesses (recesses that occur *within* a session of Congress)?[19] Or to the contrary, is it the *duration*, rather than the form, of a recess that triggers the President's authority?

The executive branch and Congress have given some of these questions consideration in Attorneys General opinions[20] and committee reports, respectively.[21] The courts, however, have rarely engaged in any significant interpretive analysis of the Clause. The Supreme Court, for example, has never considered when the President's appointment authority is triggered under the Clause, and prior to the D.C. Circuit's decision in *Noel Canning*, only three federal courts of appeals had engaged in such analyses. All three decisions arguably interpreted the Clause broadly, i.e. in a manner that imposed limited restrictions on the President's exercise of the recess appointment authority.[22] These cases are discussed in greater detail below.

The Second Circuit: *United States v. Allocco*

In the 1962 decision of *United States v. Allocco*,[23] the U.S. Court of Appeals for the Second Circuit (Second Circuit) considered a challenge to President Eisenhower's appointment of John M. Cashin as a federal judge. The position to which Judge Cashin was appointed became vacant on July 31, 1955. The Senate was in session at the time, and remained so until August 2, when it adjourned *sine die*. President Eisenhower made his appointment on August 17 during the resulting intersession recess.[24]

In determining that the President's appointment was valid, the three-judge panel unanimously held that the Recess Appointments Clause permits the filling of vacancies that "happen to exist" at the time of a recess and rejected the argument that the President cannot fill those vacancies that arise while the Senate is in session.[25] Focusing on the practical difficulties of the rejected approach, the court determined that to have adopted the more restrictive interpretation would require that offices which became vacant "on the day the senate adjourns ... remain vacant until the Senate reconvenes and has the opportunity to fill them."[26] This delay would create a "manifestly undesirable situation," "frustrate the commendable objective sought by the drafters," and "do violence to the orderly functioning of our complex government."[27] The court noted that its interpretation was "not without precedent," citing the "long and continuous line" of Attorneys General opinions determining that "the recess power extends to vacancies which arise while the Senate is in session" as well as the "widespread acceptance of [the] practice followed since the earliest days of the Republic."[28] The Second Circuit declared: "In short, a systematic, unbroken, executive practice, long pursued to the knowledge of the Congress and never before questioned, engaged in by Presidents who have also sworn to uphold the Constitution, making as it were such exercise of power part of the structure of our government, may be treated as a gloss on 'Executive Power' vested in the President by §1 of Art. II."[29]

The Ninth Circuit: *United States v. Woodley*

More than 20 years after the Second Circuit's decision, the U.S. Court of Appeals for the Ninth Circuit (Ninth Circuit) heard a similar recess appointment challenge in *United States v. Woodley*.[30] President Carter had nominated Walter Heen to be a federal district court judge on February 28, 1980. Although the Senate Judiciary Committee took up consideration of the Heen nomination, the full Senate adjourned *sine die* on December 16, 1980 without holding a confirmation vote. During the subsequent intersession recess, President Carter appointed Judge Heen pursuant to the Recess Appointments Clause on December 31, 1980.[31]

The *Woodley* court concurred with the reasoning applied in *Allocco* and held that a vacancy need not arise during a Senate recess in order to fall within the scope of the Clause.[32] In adopting the "happen to exist" interpretation of the Clause, the court noted that embracing an interpretation that did not permit the President to fill "all vacancies" that exist during a recess would lead to "absurd result[s]" and "conflict with a common sense reading of the word *happen*, as well as the construction given to this word by the three branches of our government."[33] Furthermore, a restrictive interpretation would defeat the purpose of the Clause, which the court identified as assuring to the President "the capacity for filling vacancies at any time to keep the government running smoothly."[34] Like the opinion in *Allocco*, the Ninth Circuit cited historical evidence suggesting that the executive branch has "consistently construed" the Clause as providing the President with the authority to fill any vacancy that existed at the time of the Senate recess.[35]

The Eleventh Circuit: *Evans v. Stephens*

Whereas the appointments in *Allocco* and *Woodley* were made during intersession recesses, the appointment challenged in *Evans v. Stephens*[36] was made during an intrasession recess of the Senate. On February 12, 2004, the Senate adjourned until February 23 for a "President's Day recess." During this break, President George W. Bush exercised his recess appointment power to appoint William H. Pryor to the federal bench.[37]

Citing to both *Allocco* and *Woodley*, the U.S. Court of Appeals for the Eleventh Circuit (Eleventh Circuit) interpreted the Recess Appointments Clause to "mean[] that, if vacancies 'happen' to exist during a recess, they may be filled on a temporary basis by the President."[38] The court determined that such an interpretation was "consistent with the understanding of most judges that have considered the question, written executive interpretations from as early as 1823, and legislative acquiescence."[39] The court also noted that early presidents "made recess appointments to fill vacancies that originated while the Senate was in Session."[40]

In addition, because the appointment in question had not occurred during an intersession recess, the Eleventh Circuit also became the first appellate court to hold that the Recess Appointments Clause authorized the President to make appointments during an *intrasession* recess of the Senate. The court expressly rejected the argument that the Clause "limits the opportunity to make recess appointments to one particular recess: the recess at the end of a session."[41] In adopting its interpretation, the court noted that the text of the Clause "does not differentiate expressly between inter- and intrasession recesses ..." and therefore determined that "'the Recess,' originally and through today, could just as properly refer generically to any one— intrasession or intersession— of the Senate's acts of recessing ..."[42]

The Eleventh Circuit also looked to historical practice for support, noting that 12 presidents have made over 285 intrasession recess appointments.[43] Moreover, the court identified the main purpose of the Clause as enabling "the President to fill vacancies to assure the proper functioning of our government."[44] Given this concern over administrative continuity, the court gave greater weight to the duration of the Senate recess as opposed to whether it was intersession or intrasession. The court did not, however, establish a minimum recess period required "to give legal force" to the President's recess appointment power, instead only noting that Presidents previously had made recess appointments during recesses of similar length.[45]

Thus, prior to *Noel Canning*, three federal courts of appeals had held that the President may fill any vacancy that "happens to exist" at the time of a recess, and one had concluded that the President's recess appointment authority extends to both inter- and intrasession recesses.[46] Although acknowledging that the Clause was subject to different textual interpretations, all three cases appear to have concentrated on a concern that a narrower interpretation would undermine what they identified as the overall purpose of the Clause, evidence of historical practice, and congressional acquiescence.

The January 4 Appointments

Due principally to the implementation of the aforementioned "pro forma" sessions, President Obama's recess appointments at issue in *Noel Canning* present a unique set of facts not entirely parallel to the appointments considered in *Allocco*, *Woodley*, and *Evans*. As such, prior to discussing the D.C. Circuit's decision, it is necessary to detail the January 4 appointments.

President Obama formally nominated Richard Cordray to be the first Director of the CFPB on July 18, 2011.[47] On October 6, 2011, the Senate Committee on Banking, Housing, and Urban Affairs approved Cordray's nomination for a full vote of the Senate.[48] However, on December 8, 2011, the Senate fell seven votes shy of the 60-vote threshold necessary to reach cloture and move to a vote on the nomination.[49]

The NLRB, an agency with certain powers to investigate and adjudicate unfair labor practices, consists of a board of up to five officials appointed by the President with the advice and consent of the Senate.[50] Obtaining Senate confirmation of Board nominees has been difficult in recent years.[51] Accordingly, there have been long periods during the presidencies of both George W. Bush and Obama in which the Board has had vacancies, including a period of more than two years in which the Board operated with only two Members. In 2011, the Board had only three Members—the minimum number of Members required for a quorum[52]—with one of the three scheduled to vacate his seat by the end of the first session of the 112th Congress. In an effort to prevent membership from dropping below the minimum quorum required for the Board to fully conduct business, President Obama nominated Terrence F. Flynn for a seat on the Board on January 5, 2011.[53] The President formally nominated Sharon Block and Richard F. Griffin Jr. for positions on the Board on December 15, 2011.[54] Two days later, the Senate adopted a unanimous consent agreement in which the body adjourned, but scheduled a series of "pro forma" sessions every three to four days to occur from December 20, 2011, until January 23, 2012. The unanimous consent agreement established that "no business" would be conducted during the pro forma sessions and that the second session of the 112th Congress would begin at 12:00 p.m. on January 3, 2012, as required by the Constitution.[55]

The Senate, at various times during recent Congresses, has held periodic "pro forma" sessions to "break up" what otherwise would have been a sustained adjournment. These sessions typically have been held every three or four days and are often governed by unanimous consent agreements that prohibit the chamber from conducting any formal business.[56] The sessions generally consist of a single Senator simply convening the session, assuming the chair, and then adjourning. [57]

The modern use of pro forma sessions was initially instituted in 2007 by the Senate to avoid a sustained recess with the apparent intent of preventing the President from exercising his recess appointment powers.[58] Although the purpose of the pro forma sessions has not changed, during the 112th Congress, the House began to play an active role in the implementation of the sessions. Pursuant to the Adjournments Clause, "[n]either House, during the Session of Congress, shall, without the consent of the other, adjourn for more than three days."[59] Generally then, unless both houses agree to an extended recess, neither body is constitutionally permitted to adjourn. In a June 2011 letter to House Leadership, numerous Members of the House requested that "all appropriate measures be taken to prevent any and all recess appointments by preventing the Senate from officially recessing for the remainder of the 112th Congress."[60] By refusing its consent to a Senate adjournment, the House has been able to prevent the Senate from entering into an extended recess thought necessary to trigger the President's recess appointment authority.

None of the President's four nominees were confirmed before the end of the first session of the 112th Congress. On January 4, the President, understanding the Senate to be in a recess, asserted his authority under the Recess Appointments Clause and announced his appointment of Cordray, Block, Flynn, and Griffin.[61]

D.C. CIRCUIT: *NOEL CANNING V. NLRB*

Acting with its newly appointed Members, the NLRB issued an administrative decision against Noel Canning (a Pepsi distributor and bottler) in February 2012, ruling that the company had violated the National Labor Relations Act by failing to reduce to writing a collective bargaining agreement with a local Teamsters Union. Noel Canning challenged the NLRB's decision in the D.C. Circuit, claiming that three Members of the Board were invalidly appointed and that, as a result, the Board lacked a quorum to issue the decision.[62]

A unanimous three-judge panel held that the President's three recess appointments to the Board were constitutionally invalid. The opinion rested on two alternative justifications. First, the court held that "the Recess," for purposes of the Clause, refers only to an intersession recess entered into at the end of a session of Congress pursuant to a *sine die* adjournment.[63] Second, a two-judge majority[64] held that the President may make recess appointments only to fill vacancies that arise during the intersession recess in which the appointment is made.[65] The President's recess appointments were neither made, nor did the vacancies arise, during "the Recess."

Before proceeding to a detailed discussion of the case, it may be useful to identify three key themes that appear to pervade the court's opinion. First, the opinion favors a strict textualist constitutional interpretation and endeavors to ascertain the public meaning of the Recess Appointments Clause at the time it was adopted.[66] Second, rather than adopting the historical evidence embraced in *Allocco*, *Woodley*, and *Evans*, the opinion reassessed, and arguably revalued, the historical use of recess appointments.[67] Third, the opinion invokes *Marbury v. Madison* to support the conclusion that the judiciary is the proper and ultimate arbiter for this type of constitutional dispute.[68]

"The Recess"

In holding that the President's authority to make recess appointments extends only to intersession recesses of the Senate, the D.C. Circuit placed significant importance on the Framers' choice of the phrase "the Recess," as opposed to "a recess," the plural "recesses" or the even broader "adjournment."[69] Looking to the "natural meaning of text as it would have been understood at the time of the ratification of the Constitution," the court found that the use of "the Recess," "points to the inescapable conclusion" that the Framers must have intended the Clause to mean something other than a "generic break in proceedings."[70] Moreover, the court also determined that the Clause creates a dichotomy between "the Recess" and "Session," resulting in the conclusion that "[e]ither the Senate is in session, or it is in the recess. If it has broken for three days within an ongoing session it is not in 'the Recess.'"[71] The court concluded that the only time that the Senate is not in "Session," and therefore is in "the Recess," is during the period between the termination of one session and the beginning of another.[72]

The D.C. Circuit also concluded that historical practice "strongly supports the intersession interpretation" of "the Recess."[73] However, in evaluating the historical use of the Clause, the court made clear that the "early understanding of the constitution is more probative of its original meaning than anything to be drawn from administrations of more recent vintage."[74] The court was not swayed by the prevalence of intrasession recess appointments made by recent Presidents, but rather accorded significant weight to the fact that only three intrasession recess appointments were made before 1947 and that "no President attempted to make an intrasession recess appointment for 80 years after the Constitution was ratified."[75] The court concluded that "the infrequency of intrasession recess appointments during the first 150 years of the Republic 'suggests an assumed *absence* of [the] power' to make such appointments."[76]

The Court also held that the context and purpose of the Clause buttressed its intersession interpretation. The court noted that the Clause was meant only as an appointment "stopgap" for the six- to nine-month intersession recesses of the Senate which were common at the time of the Constitution's ratification.[77] The Framers, however, placed "strict limits" on the use of the Recess authority by requiring that the appointments only be made during "the Recess."[78] "It would have made little sense to extend this 'auxillary' method to any intrasession break," held the court, "for the 'auxillary' ability to make recess appointments could easily swallow the 'general' route of advice and consent."[79]

"Vacancies That May Happen during the Recess of the Senate"

Although the D.C. Circuit's holding that recess appointments may only be made during intersession recesses was sufficient to invalidate the President's appointments, a two-judge majority also held that the President's recess appointments were invalid because the vacancies that were filled did not "happen during the Recess of the Senate."[80]

The Court determined that the Clause authorizes the President to fill only those vacancies that "come into being" or "arise" during an intersession recess, rather than those that "happen to exist" during an intersession recess.[81] Moreover, the court held that the recess appointment must occur "during the same intersession recess when the vacancy for that office arose."[82] The court arrived at this construction because a plain reading of "that may Happen" could not properly be interpreted to encompass all vacancies in existence, otherwise, the court argued, "the operative phrase ... would be wholly unnecessary."[83] The court acknowledged that this interpretation directly conflicted with the decisions in *Allocco*, *Woodley*, and *Evans*, but criticized those decisions for relying on modern dictionaries to define "happen," rather than contemporary 18th century dictionaries that would define the term as understood during the time of ratification.[84]

In support of its holding, the court also noted that a broader interpretation of "happen during the Recess" would "eviscerate the primary mode of appointments set forth in Article II, Section 2, Clause 2."[85] The court reasoned that it "would have made little sense" to impose advice and consent restrictions in the Appointments Clause when "[a] President at odds with the Senate over nominations would never have to submit his nominees for confirmation. He could simply wait for a 'recess' (however defined) and then fill up all vacancies."[86]

The court also determined that early historical commentary by Attorney General Edmund Randolph, Alexander Hamilton, and Joseph Story, suggested an early understanding that "happen" meant "arise."[87] In addition, the court noted President Washington's practice at the end of a session to obtain confirmation for a nominee, without the nominee's consent, before the Senate recess so that if the official later declined the office during the recess, the President could then fill the resulting vacancy through a recess appointment.[88]

Sine Die Adjournment

Finally, the court held that the existence of an intersession recess can be identified by the *sine die* adjournment of the Senate. Literally translated as "without day," *sine die* is a term used to describe an adjournment in which the Senate has not set a day for its next meeting[89] and is, therefore, not scheduled to meet again until the day set by the Constitution (or by law)[90] for its next session to convene.[91] These adjournments are the formal means by which Congress ends a session and are generally agreed to by *both* the House and the Senate through a concurrent resolution that explicitly characterizes the adjournment as "*sine die*."[92]

The court noted that "it has long been the practice of the Senate, dating back to the first Congress, to conclude its sessions and enter 'the Recess' with an adjournment *sine die*."[93] The decision would appear to suggest that a *sine die* adjournment is *necessary* to trigger the President's recess authority. The court expressly held that "[b]ecause the Senate did not adjourn *sine die*, it did not enter 'the Recess' between the First and Second Sessions of the 112th Congress."[94] Notably, the Court made clear that when the Senate declines to adjourn *sine die* by resolution, and instead remains in session until the start of the next session of Congress, the previous session "expire[s] simultaneously with the beginning of the" next session.[95] Consequently, it would appear that under *Noel Canning* the President's recess authority is triggered only during an intersession recess initiated pursuant to a *sine die* adjournment of the Senate.

CONFLICTS BETWEEN *NOEL CANNING AND ALLOCCO, WOODLEY,* AND *EVANS*

The D.C. Circuit's decision in *Noel Canning* contrasts with *Allocco, Woodley*, and *Evans* in a number of ways. Most prominently, of course, are the conflicts created by *Noel Canning*'s two chief holdings.[96] Whereas the Second, Ninth, and Eleventh Circuits had previously determined that the Clause authorized the President to fill any vacancy that "happens to exist" at the time of a recess, regardless of when the vacancy arose, the *Noel Canning* court took a more restrictive view of the Clause, holding that the President may only fill those offices that first become vacant during the recess in which the appointment is made. In addition, the D.C. Circuit's holding that the President's recess appointment authority is only triggered during an intersession recess, differs from the Eleventh Circuit's holding in *Evans* that the President may make recess appointments during both intersession and intrasession recesses. These differences are substantial and may provide a strong justification for the Supreme Court to grant review of this case.[97]

However, the disagreements between *Noel Canning* and the three previous appellate decisions extend beyond the ultimate scope of the President's authority under the Recess Appointments Clause. Indeed, the opinions fundamentally diverge on a number of important interpretive and practical issues. Some of these distinctions are briefly highlighted below.

Approach to Constitutional Interpretation

The opinions differed in their overall approaches to constitutional interpretation. In *Noel Canning*, the D.C. Circuit employed a formalistic textualist approach, invoking "cold, unadorned logic," in interpreting the language of the Recess Appointment Clause.[98] Seeking the plain logical meaning of the Clause, the court characterized its search as one for the "natural meaning of the text as it would have been understood at the time of the ratification of the Constitution."[99] Although also beginning with an evaluation of the Clause's text, the decisions in *Allocco*, *Woodley*, and *Evans* arguably engaged in a more functional, purpose-driven interpretation—focusing on the practical impact of a more restrictive interpretation of the Clause; its effect on the President's ability to ensure continuity of government; and the potential that a such an interpretation would "frustrate the commendable objective sought by the drafters."[100]

Purpose of the Clause

The decisions differed in their characterizations of the basic purpose of the Clause. Whereas the earlier decisions characterized the Clause as ensuring that the President be able to fill vacancies to avoid administrative inefficiency, the *Noel Canning* court viewed the Clause primarily as a "stopgap" establishing a limited exception to the general requirement that nominees be approved by the Senate.[101] Indeed, *Evans*, *Woodley*, and *Allocco* all referenced the importance of preventing "executive paralysis" or "atrophy" so as to ensure smooth functioning of government.[102] *Evans* expressly identified the purpose of the Clause as "enabl[ing] the president to fill vacancies to assure the proper functioning of our government" and "to keep important offices filled and the government functioning."[103] *Noel Canning* criticized that characterization of the Clause's purpose for "omitt[ing] a crucial element of the Clause, which enables the President to fill vacancies *only when the Senate is unable to provide advice and consent*."[104] Moreover, the D.C. Circuit noted that any "inefficiencies" that arise as a result of the court's interpretation, can be "alleviate[d]" by Congress through holdover provisions or by authorizing "acting" officers.[105]

Historical Practice

In *Allocco*, the Second Circuit supported its conclusion that a vacancy need not arise during a recess with an evaluation of historical practice. The court noted that "we find widespread acceptance of [that] practice followed since the earliest days of the Republic."[106] The *Evans* court agreed, noting that "as we understand the history, early Presidents [] made recess appointments to fill vacancies that originated while the Senate was in session."[107] As an example, the court specifically cited to an appointment made by George Washington to a vacancy that the court asserted arose while the Senate was in session.[108] *Evans* also cited historical practice in support of the conclusion that the President can make intrasession recess appointments, identifying 12 more recent presidents that had made in excess of 285 intrasession appointments.[109]

Noel Canning's evaluation of historical practice led that court to the opposite conclusion on both fronts. The court determined that in fact, "historical practice strongly supports the intersession interpretation" of the Clause.[110] The court found that the first intrasession appointment did not occur until 1867, and only three such appointments were made prior to 1947. In fact, the court noted that no president had attempted an intrasession recess appointment for the republic's first 80 years and that it has only been administrations of a "more recent vintage" that have regularly made intrasession recess appointments.[111] "The dearth of intrasession appointments in the years and decades following the ratification of the Constitution" concluded the court, "speaks far more impressively than the history of recent presidential exercise of a supposed power to make such appointments."[112]

Noel Canning also contested *Evans*'s use of historical evidence as a basis for its conclusion that Presidents may make recess appointments to any vacancy, regardless of when it arose. The D.C. Circuit challenged *Evans*'s reliance on "a handful of recess appointments supposedly made by Presidents Washington and Jefferson to offices that became vacant prior to the recess," asserting that "[s]ubsequent scholarship has demonstrated" that the cited vacancies did not actually arise while the Senate was in session.[113]

Congressional Acquiescence

Finally, the courts are in direct conflict over the import of the enactment of 5 U.S.C. §5503 and its predecessor statutes. This statutory provision, as it currently exists, provides that "[p]ayment for services *may not* be made from the Treasury of the United States to an individual appointed during a recess of the Senate to fill a vacancy in an existing office, if the vacancy existed while the Senate was in session.... "[114] The provision, however, establishes three broad exceptions to this general rule.[115]

Allocco, *Woodley*, and *Evans*, all identified this statute as a basis for implying congressional approval of the President's authority to fill vacancies that arise while the Senate is still in session. In *Allocco*, the court stated that

"Congress has implicitly recognized the President's power to fill vacancies which arise when the Senate is in session by authorizing payment of salaries to most persons so appointed under the recess power."[116] In *Woodley*, the court cited to the statute in reasoning that "[b]oth Houses of Congress have apparently recognized the soundness of this construction of the recess power" by "provid[ing] for payment of recess appointees ... whose nominations were pending at the time of the Senate's recess."[117] Likewise in *Evans*, the court explained: "That Congress is willing, under certain circumstances to pay recess appointees filling vacancies that have existed while the Senate was in session suggests to us that it is the view of the majority of Congress that the President's making of such appointments is likely not unconstitutional."[118]

The D.C. Circuit adopted a different interpretation in *Noel Canning*, concluding that the statute neither amounted to congressional acquiescence, nor provided any insight into the proper interpretation of the scope of the Recess Appointments Clause. The court questioned whether "our sister circuits are correct in construing this legislation as acquiescent," and instead concluded that the pay statute, which was first enacted in 1940 "sheds no light on the original understanding of the Constitution."[119]

NOEL CANNING'S POTENTIAL IMPACT ON THE RELATIONSHIP BETWEEN THE PRESIDENT AND CONGRESS

Although the D.C. Circuit's actual order in *Noel Canning* directly implicates only one specific action, against one specific party, within one specific circuit,[120] the court's interpretation of the President's recess appointment authority could have a substantial impact on the future division of power between the President and Congress in the filling of vacancies. If affirmed by the Supreme Court,[121] the likely effect of the reasoning adopted in *Noel Canning* would be a shift toward increased Senate control over the appointment of government officials and a decrease in the frequency of presidential recess appointments.[122] Most prominently, the President would no longer be permitted to make intrasession recess appointments. Since 1981, 329 appointments— more than half of all recess appointments made during that period—have been made during *intrasession* recesses of the Senate.[123] In addition, the President would no longer be permitted to exercise his recess appointment authority to fill vacancies that arose while the Senate was in session, or that arose during a different intersession recess. Although CRS has not been able to determine the precise number of appointments that would have fallen into this category, it would appear that few of the 323 *intersession* recess appointments made since 1981[124] filled vacancies that arose during the intersession recess in which the appointment was made.[125] Vacancies in positions requiring Senate confirmation that no longer qualify for a recess appointment under *Noel Canning* would need to be filled through the general process of presidential nomination and Senate confirmation. Thus, by limiting both the periods in which a President may make recess appointments, and the vacancies that may be filled by such appointments, the decision likely would strengthen the Senate's "Advice and Consent" role, while restricting the President's authority to make unilateral appointments.

Moreover, the interpretation established in *Noel Canning* likely would provide Congress with nearly complete control over whether the President's recess authority is triggered in the future. Under the decision, it would appear that the necessary predicate for the President to make a recess appointment (an intersession recess) must be initiated by a *sine die* adjournment of the Senate.[126] As previously noted, whether the Senate enters a *sine die* adjournment is a decision left to that body—in cooperation with the House—and one in which the President has no direct role.[127] Therefore, the Senate[128] may effectively control whether the condition necessary to trigger the President's authority to make recess appointments actually transpires. Indeed, if the Senate chooses not to adjourn *sine die* during a given Congress—a decision well within the Senate's discretion and authority—under *Noel Canning* no recess appointments may be made. This notion of Senate control over the constitutional contingency necessary to trigger the President's recess appointment authority is not, in and of itself, exceptional. In light of the conditional nature of the Clause, even the executive branch has acknowledged that "Congress can prevent the President from making any recess appointments by *remaining continuously in session and available to receive and act on nominations* ..." [129] The disagreement, however, is over how to distinguish when the Senate is in "session" and when it is in "recess." The executive argues that it is within the President's power to determine when the Senate is in "recess" for purposes of the Clause and unable to act on nominations.[130]

Under the standards established in *Noel Canning*, the Senate would also appear free to enter extended intrasession recesses without the risk of triggering the President's recess authority.[131] Neither the *duration* of a recess nor the Senate's ability to receive and weigh nominations were factors in the D.C. Circuit's consideration of what constituted "the Recess" for purposes of the Clause.[132] Instead, the court limited its evaluation only to establishing a distinction between the *form* of the recess—concluding that intersession recesses trigger the President's authority and intrasession recesses do not. As a result, it could be argued under *Noel Canning* that while the President is not permitted to make a recess appointment during a multi-month intrasession recess, he may make a recess appointment during even a momentary intersession recess—assuming that the vacancy to be filled arose during that recess.[133]

For example, *Noel Canning* would appear to suggest that the President would not be authorized to make recess appointments during a three-month summer intrasession recess. The same would also appear to be true for a properly scheduled extended intrasession recess held at the end of a session. The Senate could, for instance, adjourn on December 1st with an agreement to return on January 2.[134] Upon returning, perhaps for a pro forma session, the Senate could then adjourn that *pro forma* session, but without adjourning *sine die*. Under Senate precedent, in the absence of an explicit *sine die* adjournment, the current session of Congress would remain in being until noon on January 3, at which point *Noel Canning* makes clear that the current session would automatically "expire[] simultaneously with the beginning of the [next] session."[135] Under such a scenario the Senate would not have entered an intersession recess, and thus the President would have no opportunity to make a recess appointment.[136]

In addition to simply avoiding intersession recesses, Congress also may discourage future presidential recess appointments by structuring the terms of newly created fixed term offices in a way that decreases the likelihood that they will become vacant during an intersession recess. For example, as opposed to tying the term to the date in which the officer was appointed, Congress could establish a term of service that expires during the middle of the calendar year when the Senate is unlikely to be in an intersession recess.[137]

An argument may be forwarded that, by permitting the Senate to use scheduling practices, including pro forma sessions, to consistently prevent the President from making recess appointments, the restrictive interpretation adopted in *Noel Canning* tends to undermine the President's appointment power in a way that could give rise to constitutional concerns under the separation of powers. It would appear unlikely that the D.C. Circuit, which views the Clause as establishing a purely conditional auxiliary power, would be moved by such an argument.[138] Under its formalistic approach, the purpose of the Clause would not be frustrated simply because the required constitutional condition, identified by the Framers as necessary to trigger the

President's power, does not occur. As such, the separation of powers simply is not implicated.

By contrast, a court that adopts a more functional interpretation and identifies the primary purpose of the Clause as ensuring the President's ability to maintain the continuity of administrative government and avoid "executive paralysis" may be more receptive to such an argument.[139] A court adopting this view may consider the Senate's failure to act on nominations, coupled with a restrictive interpretation of the President's authority to make recess appointments, as unduly obstructing the President's ability to "take Care that the Laws be faithfully executed"[140] and frustrating what some courts have identified as the overriding objective of the Clause: to allow the President to "fill vacancies to assure the proper functioning of our government."[141]

In discussing the boundaries of the constitutional roles of each branch, it should be noted that recess appointments have been governed by a delicate balance of power precisely because the Clause establishes a unique affirmative grant of constitutional power to one branch that is conditional upon the occurrence of a specific action of another. The structure of the appointment process, and the ability of either branch to exercise its enumerated authority in a manner that frustrates the powers of the other branch, has resulted in a framework traditionally governed by political checks and balances, rather than strict legal standards, and is perhaps why substantial ambiguity as to the scope of the Clause persists to this day. Any judicial decision providing additional legal clarity to the question of who determines whether the Senate is in "the Recess" runs the risk of upsetting this balance of power. If the authority to make this determination is accorded to the President, the resulting dynamic could significantly undermine the Senate's advice and consent role under the Appointments Clause. If the decision-making power is accorded to the Senate, the President conceivably could be prevented from making any recess appointments, regardless of the resulting impact on the functioning of the executive branch. If the former would "eviscerate the Constitution's separation of powers," as the *Noel Canning* court concluded, it would seem the same argument could be made of the latter.[142]

Finally, it should be noted that although the President has very little control over when and whether the Senate enters an intersession recess of the type required in *Noel Canning*,[143] he may be able to influence the timing of certain executive branch vacancies. For example, if the Senate enters an intersession recess, the President may attempt to create a vacancy during that period by encouraging certain officers who have determined to leave the administration to time their resignations to coincide with the Senate recess. In addition, depending on the statutory protections afforded a given office, the President could remove an officer during the intersession recess, thus creating a vacancy that could be filled via a recess appointment.[144] Of course, this method would allow the President to create a vacancy only in an already occupied office and would have no impact on offices that are *already* vacant or newly established.[145]

The Adjournments Clause and the Role of the House

The *Noel Canning* decision also could impact the House's ability to influence the President's recess appointment authority. As previously discussed, the Adjournments Clause establishes that "neither House, during the Session of Congress, shall without the consent of the other, adjourn for more than three days."[146] By withholding its consent to an extended Senate recess in recent years, the House has effectively prevented the Senate from entering a recess of a length generally thought sufficient to permit the President to exercise his recess appointment authority.

Prior to *Noel Canning* it was generally thought that a recess of some appreciable length likely was necessary to trigger the President's recess appointment authority.[147] At the very least, the executive branch has drawn from the Adjournments Clause to assert that a recess would likely need to be "longer than 3 days" in order for a recess appointment to be made, although early legal opinions favored a longer period.[148] Given this perceived durational requirement, the Adjournments Clause arguably prevented the Senate from entering a recess of sufficient length to trigger the President's recess authority without the consent of the House. *Noel Canning* appears to suggest that this perception was in error. Not only did the circuit court explicitly determine that the asserted "link" between the Adjournments Clause and the Recess Appointments Clause "lack[ed] any constitutional basis," nothing in the opinion suggested that "the Recess" needs to be of some minimum duration for recess appointments to be made.[149] Regardless of the length of a recess, so long as it is intersession (adjourned *sine die*), *Noel Canning* suggests that the President's recess appointment authority is triggered.

Given these new developments, it can be argued that the House's ability to influence the President's authority to make recess appointments in the future could be weakened were the Senate willing to break from its tradition of obtaining the House's consent for a *sine die* adjournment.[150] The Adjournments Clause requires the Senate to obtain the consent of the House only to "adjourn for more than three days." Thus, there does not appear to be any constitutional reason why the Senate would not be free to unilaterally enter an intersession recess within three days of the convening of the next session without the consent of the House. In practice, this is not an action the Senate has historically taken,[151] and indeed would appear to be contrary to Senate precedent.[152] Nevertheless, under *Noel Canning*, this short intersession recess would appear to be sufficient to trigger the President's recess appointment power.

End Notes

[1] The Supreme Court has distinguished "principal officers," who must be appointed by the President with the advice and consent of the Senate, from inferior officers, whose appointment Congress may vest solely in the President, the judiciary, or a head of a department. U.S. Const. art. II, §2, cl. 2 ("[H]e shall nominate, and by and with the Advice and Consent of the Senate, shall appoint Ambassadors, other public Ministers and Consuls, Judges of the supreme Court, and all other Officers of the United States, whose Appointments are not herein otherwise provided for, and which shall be established by Law: but the Congress may by Law vest the Appointment of such inferior Officers, as they think proper, in the President alone, in the Court of Law, or in the Heads of Departments.").

[2] U.S. Const. art. II, §2, cl. 3.

[3] CRS Report RL33009, *Recess Appointments: A Legal Overview*, by Vivian S. Chu, at 2 (citing numerous examples of contentious recess appointments).

[4] 157 CONG. REC. S883-S8784 (daily ed. Dec. 17, 2011). Under the Twentieth Amendment, each new session of Congress is required to begin "at noon on the 3d day of January, unless [Congress] shall by law appoint a different day." U.S. Const. Amend XX §2.

[5] *President Obama Announces Recess Appointments to Key Administration Posts*, White House, Press Release, Jan. 4, 2012, available at http://www.whitehouse.gov/the-press-office/2012/01/04/president-obama-announces-recess- appointments-key-administration-posts.

[6] See Lyle Denniston, *Spreading challenge to appointment power (UPDATED)*, SCOTUSblog, Jan. 28, 2013, available at http://www.scotusblog.com/2013/01/spreading-challenge-to-appointment-power/; Complaint, State Nat'l Bank of Big Spring v. Geithner, Case No. 1:12-cv-01032 (D.C. Sept. 20, 2012), available at http://newsandinsight.thomsonreuters.com/uploadedFiles/Reuters_Content/2012/09_-_September/statenationvcfpb—amendedcomplaint.pdf; Opposition to Receiver's Second Request for Payment, Consumer Fin. Prot. Bureau v. Gordon, Case No. CV12-6147-RSWL(MRWx), (C.D.Cal. July 18, 2012), available at http://www.cfpbmonitor.com/files/ 2013/ 02/CGCFPB-Opp-Rec-Req-2.pdf.

[7] No. 12-115 (D.C. Cir., Jan. 25, 2013) (hereinafter *Noel Canning*) available at http://www.cadc.uscourts.gov/internet/opinions.nsf/D13E4C2A7B33B57A85257AFE00556B29/$file/12-1115- 1417096.pdf.

[8] *Id.* at 30, 44.

[9] Taken to its logical limits, the reasoning of the opinion could create uncertainty as to the validity of hundreds of other recess appointments made across the government in recent years. Consideration of these appointments is beyond the scope of this report.

[10] U.S. Const. art. II, §2, cl. 2.

[11] Once confirmed by the Senate, an officer is not formally appointed until his commission is signed by the President.

[12] U.S. Const. art. II, §2, cl. 3.

[13] M. Ferrand, *Records of the Federal Convention of 1787*, at 533, 540, 574, 600 (rev. ed. 1966). The Clause does not appear to have been discussed during the Constitutional Convention. The language was first drafted in Hamilton's plan of government, adopted upon the motion of Richard Spaight of North Carolina, and left unchanged by the Committee of Style. *Id.* Moreover, "the contemporaneous writings of the Framers are virtually barren of any references to the Recess Appointments Clause." U.S. v. Woodley, 751 F.2d 1008, 1017 (9th Cir. 1985).

[14] The Federalist, No. 67, at 409-10 (Alexander Hamilton) (Clinton Rossiter ed. 1961).

[15] Hamilton addressed the purpose of the Clause in response to an assertion that the language authorized the President to fill vacancies of the Senate. *Id.*

[16] Evans v. Stephens, 387 F.3d 1220, 1223 (11th Cir. 2004).

[17] *Id.* See also Staebler v. Carter, 464 F. Supp. 585, 597 (D.D.C. 1979) ("There is nothing to suggest that the Recess Appointments Clause was designed as some sort of extraordinary and lesser method of appointment ...).

[18] See 41 Op. A.G. 463, 470-471 (1960); 28 Comp. Gen. 121 (1948). In contrast, a confirmed appointee will serve at the pleasure of the President or subject to the term of office prescribed by statute. CRS Report RL33009, *Recess Appointments: A Legal Overview*, by Vivian S. Chu.

[19] It should be noted that prior to the Civil War intrasession recesses were relatively uncommon as Congress generally met for relatively short sessions followed by long intersession recesses of six to nine months.

[20] For example, aspects of the recess appointments power were considered as early as 1792, and there were at least 19 formal Attorneys General opinions in the 19th century on recess appointments, the earliest written in 1823. CRS Report RL33009, *Recess Appointments: A Legal Overview*, by Vivian S. Chu.

[21] See, e.g. S.Rept. 58-4389 at 2 (1905) ("[Recess] means, in our judgment, in this connection the period of time when the Senate is *not sitting in regular or extraordinary session as a branch of the Congress* ...; when its members owe no duty of attendance; when its Chamber is empty; when, because of its absence, it can not [*sic*] receive communications from the President or participate as a body in making appointments.") (emphasis in original).

[22] All three cases arose in the context of judicial appointments, and all three courts also held that the Recess Appointments Clause authorized the President to fill judicial vacancies.

[23] 305 F.2d 704 (2nd Cir. 1962).

[24] *Id.* at 705.

[25] *Id.* at 710-13.

[26] *Id.* at 710.

[27] *Id.* The court also recognized that the entire process from selection to confirmation "frequently consumes many months." If the President was only able to fill vacancies that arose during a Senate recess, the process of selecting and confirming a nominee for a vacancy that arose near the end of a Senate session would have to be "telescoped into whatever time remains in a session.... " *Id.* at 711-12.

[28] *Id.* at 713.

[29] *Id.* at 714 (quoting Youngstown Sheet & Tube Co. v. Sawyer, 343 U.S. 579, 610-11 (1952) (Frankfurter, J. concurring)).

[30] 751 F.2d 1008 (9th Cir. 1985)

[31] *Id.* at 1009.

[32] 751 F.2d 1008 (9th Cir. 1985).

[33] *Id.* at 1012.

[34] *Id.* at 1013 (citing *Allocco*, 305 F.2d at 712).

[35] *Id.* Although 11 of the 15 judges involved in the en banc appeal joined the majority opinion, four judges issued a dissent that strongly criticized the majority's "reliance upon the executive's practice" in interpreting the meaning of the Clause. *Id.* at 1015 (Norris, J. dissenting).

[36] 387 F.3d 1220 (11th Cir. 2004).

[37] *Id.* at 1222. Judge Pryor was appointed to the U.S. Court of Appeals for the Eleventh Circuit and recused himself from review of his own appointment.

[38] *Id.* at 1225.

[39] *Id.* at 1226.

[40] *Id.* The court specifically highlighted appointments made by Presidents Washington and Jefferson.

[41] *Id.* at 1224.

[42] *Id.* at 1224-25.

[43] *Id.* at 1226 ("Twelve Presidents have made more than 285 intrasession recess appointments of persons to offices that ordinarily require consent of the Senate. So, given the words of the Constitution and the history, we are unpersuaded by the argument that the recess appointment power may only be used in an intersession recess, but not an intrasession recess.").

[44] *Id.* The court added: "The purpose of the Clause is no less satisfied during an intrasession recess than during a recess of potentially even shorter duration that comes as an intersession break." *Id.*

[45] *Id.* at 1225. In dissent, Judge Barkett determined that "the plain meaning of the Recess Appointments Clause directly, expressly, and unambiguously requires that before a vacancy can be filled through the recess appointment power, that vacancy must have occurred during a Senate recess." Although he would not have reached the question of whether "the Recess" encompasses both intersession and intrasession recesses, Judge Barkett suggested that "the text of the Constitution as well as the weight of the historical record strongly suggest that the Founders meant to denote only intersession recesses."

[46] There also have been several district court opinions on the topic. See, e.g., Staebler v. Carter, 464 F.Supp.585 (D.D.C. 1979); Gould v. United States, 19 Ct. Cl. 593, 595-96 (1884).

[47] 157 CONG. REC. S4646 (daily ed. July 18, 2011). Title X of the Dodd-Frank Wall Street Reform and Consumer Protection Act established the CFPB and provided the independent agency with rulemaking, enforcement, and supervisory powers over many consumer financial products and services, as well as the entities that provide them.

[48] *Johnson Statement on Committee Approval of Richard Cordray's Nomination to Lead the CFPB*, S. Comm. on Banking, Hous., and Urban Affairs, Press Release, Oct. 6, 2011, available at http://shelby.senate.gov/public/index.cfm/ newsreleases?ContentRecord_id =893bc8b0-2e73-4555-8441-d51e0ccd1d17.

[49] 157 CONG. REC. S8429 (daily ed. Dec. 8, 2011). In May 2011, 44 Senators signed a letter to the President stating that they would oppose the confirmation of any nominee to serve as CFPB Director until substantive changes to the structure of the Bureau were enacted into law. *44 U.S. Sen. to Obama: No Accountability, No Confirmation*, Sen. Richard Shelby, News Release, May 5, 2011, available at http://shelby.senate.gov/public/index.cfm/2011/5/ 44-u-s- sens-to-obama-no-accountability-no-confirmation.

[50] 29 U.S.C. §153.

[51] Indeed, five of the last seven appointments to the Board have been recess appointments. See *Members of the NLRB since 1935*, available at http://www.nlrb.gov/members-nlrb-1935.

[52] In 2010, the Supreme Court ruled that the National Labor Relations Act prevents the NLRB from exercising rulemaking powers without having three or more acting Members. New Process Steel v. Nat'l Labor Relations Bd., 130 S. Ct. 2635 (2010).

[53] 157 CONG. REC. S68 (daily ed. Jan. 5, 2011).

[54] 157 CONG. REC.. S8691 (daily ed. Dec. 15, 2011). President Obama had nominated Craig Becker on January 26, 2011 to retain the seat on the Board that he had previously held by recess appointment. That nomination was withdrawn on December 15, 2011. *Id.*

[55] 157 CONG. REC.. S883-S8784 (daily ed. Dec. 17, 2011). The unanimous consent agreement stated that the Senate would "adjourn and convene for pro forma sessions only, with no business conducted" on December 20, 23, 27, and 30; that the second session of the 112th Congress would convene on January 3 at noon "for a pro forma session only, with no business conducted;" and that the Senate would then convene for pro forma sessions "with no business conducted" on January 6, 10, 13, 17, and 20, 2012.

[56] Despite the agreement that no business would be conducted, the Senate approved the Temporary Payroll Tax Cut Continuation Act of 2011by unanimous consent on December 23, 2011. 157 Cong. Rec. S8789 (daily ed., December 23, 2011).

[57] Pro forma sessions are generally short in duration, often lasting no more than a few minutes. See 158 CONG. REC.S1 (daily ed. Jan. 3, 2012).

[58] In November 2007, the Senate Majority Leader announced that the Senate would "be coming in for pro forma sessions during the Thanksgiving holiday to prevent recess appointments" as it was thought that a recess of three days or less was insufficient to trigger the Presidents recess authority. 153 CONG. REC.. S14698 (daily ed., Nov. 16, 2007). The development of this practice is perhaps informed by existing statements of the Department of Justice that link the Recess Appointments Clause to the Adjournment Clause. However, it also appears that the use of pro forma sessions to prevent recess appointments was at least contemplated as early as the 1980s. See CRS Congressional Distribution Memorandum, "Efforts to Prevent Recess Appointments through Congressional Scheduling and Historical Recess Appointments During Short Intervals Between Sessions," by Henry Hogue and Richard Beth (October 24, 2011) (hereinafter CRS Recess Appointments Memorandum).

[59] U.S. Const. art. I, §5, cl. 4.

[60] *Letter to the Speaker of the House John Boehner, et al.*, June 15, 2011. Neither the House nor the Senate had introduced a concurrent resolution of adjournment from May 12, 2011, until January 3, 2012. A similar letter addressed to House leadership was signed by a group of Senators on May 25, 2011. *Vitter, DeMint Urge House to Block Controversial Recess Appointments*, U.S. Sen. David Vitter, Press Release, May 25, 2011.

[61] *President Obama Announces Recess Appointments to Key Administration Posts*, White House, Press Release, Jan. 4, 2012, available at http://www.whitehouse.gov/the-press-office/2012/01/04/president-obama-announces-recess- appointments-key-administration-posts. The appointments occurred in the time between pro forma sessions on January 3 and January 6, 2012.

[62] Noel Canning v. National Labor Relations Bd., No. 12-1115 (D.C. Cir. Jan. 25, 2013).

[63] *Id.* at 16-30. It should be noted that the court's discussion of the importance of a *sine die* adjournment, although applicable to both parts of the opinion, occurred within the portion of the opinion that Judge Griffith did not find necessary. *Id.* at 40-43.

[64] Noting that the "intersession recess" holding was sufficient to invalidate the appointments, Judge Griffith did not join the court's holding that a vacancy also must arise during "the Recess." *Id.* at 47 (Griffith, J. concurring) ("I agree that the Executive's view that the President can fill vacancies that 'happen to exist' during 'the Recess' is suspect, but that position dates back to at least the 1820s, making it more venerable than the much more recent practice of intrasession recess appointments. We should not dismiss another branch's longstanding interpretation of the Constitution when the case before us does not demand it.") (internal citations omitted).

[65] *Id.* at 30-39.

[66] See, e.g., *id.* at 17 ("When interpreting a constitutional provision, we must look to the natural meaning of the text as it would have been understood at the time of the ratification of the Constitution.").

[67] See, e.g., *id.* at 19-20 ("In fact, the historical role of the Recess Appointments Clause is neither clear nor consistent."); *Id.* at 21 ("[W]e conclude that practice of a more recent vintage is less compelling than historical practice dating back to the era of the Framers.").

[68] See, e.g., *id.* at 29 ("While we recognize that all branches of government must of necessity exercise their understanding of the Constitution in order to perform their duties faithfully thereto, ultimately it is our role to discern the authoritative meaning of the supreme law.").

[69] *Id.* at 16-18.

[70] *Id.* at 17.

[71] *Id.* at 17-18.

[72] *Id.* at 18 ("It is universally accepted that 'Session' here refers to the usually two or sometimes three sessions per Congress. Therefore, 'the Recess' should be taken to mean only times when the Senate is not in one of those sessions.").

[73] *Id.* at 20.

[74] *Id.* at 21, 29 ("The dearth of intrasession appointments in the years and decades following the ratification of the Constitution speaks far more impressively than the history of recent presidential exercise of a supposed power to make such appointments.").

[75] *Id.* at 20.

[76] *Id.* at 21(emphasis in original). Although the court acknowledged that the hardships of travel made intrasession recesses of any significant length quite rare in early Congresses, the court nonetheless asserted that "the appointment practices of Presidents more nearly contemporaneous with the adoption of the Constitution do not support the propriety of intrasession recess appointments." *Id.*

[77] *Id.* at 22.

[78] *Id.* at 23.

[79] *Id.*

[80] *Id.* at 30-44. The court began its analysis "by looking at the natural meaning of the text as it would have been understood at the time of the ratification of the Constitution." *Id.* at 30-31.

[81] *Id.* at 30-31. ("Upon a simple reading of the language itself, we conclude that the word 'happen' could not logically have encompassed any vacancies that happened to exist during 'the Recess.'").

[82] *Id.* at 43-44.

[83] *Id.* at 31.

[84] *Id.* at 35-36.

[85] *Id.* at 32.

[86] *Id.*

[87] *Id.* at 33-35.

[88] *Id.* at 33 ("If President Washington and the early Senate had understood the word 'happen' to mean 'happen to exist,' this convoluted process would have been unnecessary.").

[89] For a more detailed discussion of *sine die* adjournment and Senate scheduling practices implemented to prevent presidential recess appointments, see CRS Recess Appointments Memorandum, *supra* note 58. See also CRS Report R42977, *Sessions, Adjournments, and Recesses of Congress*, by Richard S. Beth and Jessica Tollestrup, at 10-11.

[90] U.S. Const. amend XX §2 ("The Congress shall assemble at least once in every year, and such meeting shall begin at noon on the 3d day of January, unless they shall by law appoint a different day.").

[91] The opinion did not address the effect a conditional *sine die* adjournment would have on the President's authority to make recess appointments. Under this type of adjournment, the Senate adjourns *sine die*, but leaves open the possibility that the body will choose to reconvene at some point prior to the scheduled start of the next session.

[92] For a discussion of the rare instances since the ratification of the Twentieth Amendment in which a session of the Senate was finally adjourned without a concurrent resolution of *sine die* adjournment, see CRS Recess Appointments Memorandum, *supra* note 58.

[93] *Noel Canning,* No. 12-115, at 40.

[94] *Id.* at 43.

[95] *Id.* at 42 ("Because, in this case, the Senate declined to adjourn *sine die* on December 30, 2011, it did not enter an intersession recess, and the First Session of the 112th Congress expired simultaneously with the beginning of the Second Session.").

[96] It should be noted that the decisions of other circuits have no binding precedential effect within the D.C. Circuit. As such the court was under no obligation to give weight to the conclusions of the Second, Ninth, and Eleventh Circuits.

[97] The NLRB has announced its intent to appeal the decision to the Supreme Court. NLRB To Seek Supreme Court Review in Noel Canning v. NLRB, NLRB News Release March 12, 2013.

[98] *Noel Canning*, No. 12-115 at 17.

[99] *Id.* at 30.

[100] See, e.g., *Allocco*, 305 F.2d at 710 ("If we were to adopt the petitioner's interpretation, by reading the word 'happened' as if it is suspended in space without any history, context, or purpose, we would frustrate the commendable objective sought by the drafters.").

[101] *Noel Canning*, at 22.

[102] *Evans*, 387 F.3d at 1235; *Woodley*, 751 F.2d at 1013 ("The clause prevents the Executive from being incapacitated during the recess of the Senate."); *Allocco*, 305 F.2d at 712.

[103] *Evans*, 387 F.3d at 1226.

[104] *Noel Canning*, at 26 (emphasis in original).

[105] *Id.* at 37-38.

[106] *Allocco*, 305 F.2d at 713.

[107] *Evans*, 387 F.3d at 1226.

[108] *Id.* at 1226.

[109] *Id.* ("Twelve Presidents have made more than 285 intrasession recess appointments of persons to offices that ordinarily require consent of the Senate.").

[110] *Noel Canning*, at 20.

[111] *Id.* at 21

[112] *Id.* at 29.

[113] *Id.* at 35 (citing Michael B. Rappaport, *The Original Meaning of the Recess Appointments Clause,* 52 UCLA L. Rev. 1487, 1522, n.97 (2005)).

[114] 5 U.S.C. §5503 (emphasis added).

[115] The provision does not apply: "(1) if the vacancy arose within 30 days before the end of the session of the Senate; (2) if, at the end of the session, a nomination for the office, other than the nomination of an individual appointed during the preceding recess of the Senate, was pending before the Senate for its advice and consent; or (3) if a nomination for the office was rejected by the Senate within 30 days before the end of the session and an individual other than the one whose nomination was rejected thereafter receives a recess appointment." 5 U.S.C. §5503(a).

[116] *Allocco*, 305 F.2d at 714.

[117] *Woodley*, 751 F.2d at 1013.

[118] *Evans*, 387 F.3d at 1227, n.11.

[119] *Noel Canning*, at 36. Another court, however, has noted that "[t]he origins of the modern Vacancies Act go back to the beginning of the nation." Doolin Sec. Sav. Bank, F.S.B v. Office of Thrift Supervision, 139 F.3d 203, 209-210 (D.C. Cir. 1998).

[120] The decision carries precedential value only within the D.C. Circuit and in no way binds other federal courts outside of the circuit. In making future recess appointments, the Obama Administration—which has stated that it disagrees with the *Noel Canning* decision—may not feel bound by the restrictions established by the circuit court until the Supreme Court takes a position on the issue. See e.g., Donovan Slack, *White house Blasts Recess Appointments Ruling*, Politico, Jan. 27, 2013. However, a plaintiff challenging a future recess appointment to a position located within the District of Columbia would likely have

the choice of filing that lawsuit in the D.C. Circuit where *Noel Canning* would be accorded significant precedential weight.

[121] The NLRB has stated that it intends to file a petition for certiorari with the Supreme Court by April 25, 2013. *NLRB To Seek Supreme Court Review in Noel Canning v. NLRB*, NLRB News Release March 12, 2013.

[122] For a discussion of the decision's potential impact on the functioning of the NLRB and the CFPB see CRS Report, *Practical Implications of Noel Canning on the NLRB and CFPB*, by David Carpenter and Todd Garvey.

[123] See CRS Congressional Distribution Memorandum, *The Noel Canning Decision and Recess Appointments Made from 1981-2013*, by Henry B. Hogue, Maeve P. Carey, Michael W. Greene, and Maureen Bearden (February 4, 2013).

[124] *Id.* ("Preliminary research suggests ... that many of the intersession recess appointments listed in this memorandum might have been precluded.").

[125] This limitation also would appear to preclude two common types of recess appointments that generally do not fill vacancies that arise during the same recess in which the President makes the appointment: successive recess appointments to a single office; and the replacement of a "holdover" official with a recess appointee. See CRS Report RL33009, *Recess Appointments: A Legal Overview*, by Vivian S. Chu.

[126] *Noel Canning,* at 42 ("Because the Senate did not adjourn *sine die*, it did not enter 'the Recess' between the First and Second Sessions of the 112th Congress.").

[127] See the discussion of Article II, §3 *infra* note 143.

[128] Although the Senate may avoid an intersession recess through proper scheduling, in order to actually enter an intersession recess of more than three days, the body would need to obtain the consent of the House.

[129] 36 Op. O.L.C., at 17 (emphasis added) ("We conclude that while Congress can prevent the President from making any recess appointments by remaining continuously in session and available to receive and act on nominations, it cannot do so by conducting pro forma sessions during a recess.").

[130] See *Lawfulness of Recess Appointments During a Recess of the Senate Notwithstanding Periodic Pro Forma Sessions*, 6 Op. O.L.C. 1, 9 (2012) ("We believe that Congress's provision for pro forma sessions of this sort does not have the legal effect of interrupting the recess of the Senate for purposes of the Recess Appointments Clause and that the President may properly conclude that the Senate is unavailable for the overall duration of the recess."); Executive Power-Recess Appointments, 33 Op. Att'y Gen. 20, 25 (1921) ("I think the President is necessarily vested with a large, although not unlimited, discretion to determine when there is a real and genuine recess making it impossible for him to receive the advice and consent of the Senate.").

[131] Pursuant to the Adjournments Clause (discussed below), the Senate would need to obtain the consent of the House before adjourning for an intrasession recess that lasts more than three days. However, if it is determined that the President cannot make appointments during intrasession recesses, the House may be more willing to consent to such recesses.

[132] *Noel Canning*, at 30 ("In short, we hold that "the Recess" is limited to intersession recesses.").

[133] The facts underlying the *Noel Canning* decision did not require a holding regarding the requisite duration of a recess. If the appropriate facts underlying a subsequent challenge to a recess appointment were to come before the D.C. Circuit, the court very well may elaborate on whether the duration of the recess is a factor in considering whether the Senate is in "the Recess." It may be instructive, however, that unlike the *Evans* opinion, the *Noel Canning* opinion did not raise or identify the durational requirement in any manner.

[134] Such a recess would again require House consent. If, however, the House refused its consent, the Senate could hold pro forma sessions every three days from the date of adjournment until January 2.

[135] *Noel Canning*, at 42.

[136] The DOJ identified this point in a brief to the U.S. Court of Appeals for the Third Circuit: "... under *Noel Canning*, whether the President may act depends on how the Senate frames its adjournment, empowering the Senate unilaterally to eliminate the President's recess appointment authority even when it is unavailable to advise and consent. If the Senate adopts a resolution adjourning *sine die* ..., the adjournment ends the Senate's enumerated session, and the ensuing recess is an intersession one lasting until the start date set by law for the next session—usually January 3. If the Senate adjourns for the same period, but the resolution instead specifies a return date for that session that is immediately before the next session (say January 2), the adjournment does not end the session, and the recess is intrasession." *DOJ Supplemental Letter Brief*, Nat'l Labor Relations Bd. v. New Vista Nursing and Rehabilitation, Nos. 11-3440, 12-1027, 12-1936, at 10 (3rd Cir. Feb. 28, 3013) (internal citations omitted).

[137] Notably, this approach would not be applicable to federal judges or other executive branch officers, such as cabinet officials, who serve at the pleasure of the President for indefinite terms.

[138] *Noel Canning*, at 22-23,

[139] *Evans*, 387 F.3d, at 1235.

[140] U.S. Const. art. II §3.

[141] *Evans*, 387 F.3d, at 1225.

[142] *Noel Canning*, at 25.

[143] An argument could be forwarded that in order to counter a Senate that scheduled its recesses in a manner that prevented recess appointments, the President could exercise the authority vested in him by the Constitution to force an adjournment of the Senate and, thereby, create an intersession recess during which the President could make recess appointments. Although it appears that this adjournment power has never been exercised, Article II, §3 provides that the President "may, on extraordinary Occasions, convene both Houses, or either of them, and in Case of Disagreement between them, with respect to the Time of Adjournment, he may adjourn them to such Time as he shall think proper.... " An attempt by the President to force a Senate recess in order to make recess appointments would raise a plethora of constitutional questions, including how, and by whom, it is determined that the House and Senate are in "disagreement ... with respect to the Time of Adjournment." These questions notwithstanding, two points gleaned from *Noel Canning* are worth noting in relation to this argument. First, the decision drew a clear distinction between an "adjournment" and "the Recess": the former constituting a general term referring to any "legislative break," and the latter a specific type of adjournment between legislative sessions triggering the President's recess appointment authority. *Noel Canning*, at 27-8. If the President were to "adjourn" the Senate, the resulting "adjournment" would not necessarily constitute "the Recess" for purposes of the Clause. Moreover, *Noel Canning* suggests that the required intersession recess must be triggered by a *sine die* adjournment of the Senate. *Noel Canning*, at 40-2. Although a forced Senate adjournment pursuant to Article II would create an intersession recess, it would appear to be an open question as to whether the *Noel Canning* court would consider the resulting recess one sufficient to trigger the President's recess appointment power.

[144] Life-tenured judges and officers who enjoy removal protections likely could not be removed in such a manner.

[145] "It should be noted that one potential result of narrowing the President's recess appointment authority could be greater reliance on the Vacancies Reform Act, which authorizes the President to fill many advice and consent positions (though, notably, not those on collegial bodies such as boards and commissions) on a temporary basis. The executive branch may also increasingly rely on specific statutory provisions that permit a government official, who has not received Senate confirmation for that position, to perform the functions of an office on an acting basis. See CRS Report RS21412, *Temporarily Filling Presidentially Appointed, Senate-Confirmed Positions*, by Henry B. Hogue. For example, in the absence of

a Senate confirmed director, Edward DeMarco has served as the acting director of the Federal Housing Finance Agency since the former Director resigned in 2009. See, 12 U.S.C. §4512(f) ("In the event of the death, resignation, sickness, or absence of the Director, the President shall designate either the Deputy Director of the Division of Enterprise Regulation, the Deputy Director of the Division of Federal Home Loan Bank Regulation, or the Deputy Director for Housing Mission and Goals, to serve as acting Director until the return of the Director, or the appointment of a successor pursuant to subsection (b).").

[146] U.S. Const. art. I, §5, cl. 4.

[147] Recess appointments have, however, previously been made during short intersession recesses in at least two situations. President Truman made a recess appointment to the Civil Aeronautics Board during a three-day intersession recess in 1949. In a more controversial action, President Theodore Roosevelt made over 160 recess appointments during the "brief pause" between the end of the first session of the 58th Congress and the start of the second session in 1903. In response, the Senate Committee on the Judiciary issued a report in 1905 objecting to the appointments. S.Rept. 58-4389. For additional information on these appointments, see CRS Recess Appointments Memorandum.

[148] See Memorandum of Points and Authorities in Support of Defendants' Opposition to Plaintiffs' Motion for Partial Summary Judgment, at 24-26, Mackie v. Clinton, 827 F. Supp. 56 (D.D.C. 1993) ("If the recess here at issue were of three days or less, a closer question would be presented. The Constitution restricts the Senate's ability to adjourn its session for more than three days without obtaining the consent of the House of Representatives. It might be argued that the Framers did not consider one, two and three day recesses to be constitutionally significant."); 33 Op. Atty. Gen. 20, 24 (1921) (While declaring that the President had the authority to make a recess appointment during an intrasession recess of 29 days, Attorney General Daughtery explained his opinion did not imply that "the power exists if the adjournment is for only 2 instead of 28 days.... Nor do I think an adjournment for 5 or even 10 days can be said to constitute the recess intended by the Constitution."). Notwithstanding these statements, the OLC in its January 2012 opinion noted: "This Office has not formally concluded that there is a lower limit to the duration of a recess within which the President can make recess appointment." 36 Op. O.L.C. *9, n.13 (2012).

[149] *Noel Canning*, at 25 ("Nothing in the text of either Clause, the Constitution's structure, or its history suggests a link between the Clauses.").

[150] See CRS Recess Appointments Memorandum (noting that "it appears ... that an adjournment of this nature would be outside the usual practices of the Senate.").

[151] On at least one occasion, the Senate has unilaterally adjourned *sine die* and entered an intersession recess of less than three days without the consent of the House. In 1996, the Senate entered a three-minute intersession recess between the first and second sessions of the 104th Congress without adopting a concurrent resolution. *Id.* at 10-11.

[152] See CRS Report R42977, *Sessions, Adjournments, and Recesses of Congress*, by Richard S. Beth and Jessica Tollestrup, at 11. ("The Senate has explicitly established that, except at the point when the following session is immediately going to convene, a daily adjournment never brings about a sine die adjournment de facto, even if it occurs within three days of the convening of the next session and the body has agreed not to meet again until that next session convenes. In such a case, the Senate treats its previous session as remaining in being until the point at which the chair declares the new session to have convened. It is not clear whether, in similar circumstances, the House might by daily adjournment achieve an adjournment sine die at any earlier point within three days.").

In: Recess Appointment Power
Editor: Chase N. Morrison

ISBN: 978-1-62948-675-8

Chapter 2

PRACTICAL IMPLICATIONS OF *NOEL CANNING* ON THE NLRB AND CFPB*

David H. Carpenter and Todd Garvey

SUMMARY

In *Noel Canning v. National Labor Relations Board*, the U.S. Court of Appeals for the District of Columbia Circuit (D.C. Circuit) ruled that President Obama's appointments of three Members to the National Labor Relations Board (NLRB) were constitutionally invalid. In reaching its decision, the D.C. Circuit concluded that under the Recess Appointments Clause, the President may only make recess appointments during a formal intersession recess (a recess between the end of one session of Congress and the start of another), *and* only to fill those vacancies that arose during the intersession recess in which the appointment was made.

The legal reasoning of the case, if adopted by other courts or affirmed by the Supreme Court, could significantly alter the relationship between the President and the Congress in the appointments context. It also would cast serious doubt upon an array of previous actions by the NLRB and its ability to function in the future. Furthermore, because Richard Cordray was appointed as

---

* This is an edited, reformatted and augmented version of a Congressional Research Service publication, CRS Report for Congress R43032, dated April 1, 2013.

Director of the Bureau of Consumer Financial Protection (CFPB) at the same time and in the same manner as the NLRB appointees, *Noel Canning* raises questions about the validity of Cordray's appointment; the validity of various actions already undertaken by the CFPB; and the authority of the CFPB to function going forward.

However, the opinion's immediate impact on the functioning of the Board may be limited because the D.C. Circuit's order in *Noel Canning* vacated only the Board's administrative ruling that the company had engaged in an unfair labor practice. The decision did not invalidate any other Board actions, nor did the court issue an injunction preventing Board Members from taking any specific actions in the future. Moreover, the decision only carries precedential value within the D.C. Circuit and in no way binds other federal courts outside of the circuit.

This report assesses the potential legal impact *Noel Canning* may have on the past and future operations of the NLRB and the CFPB.

A companion report, *The Recess Appointment Power After Noel Canning v. NLRB: Constitutional Implications*, by Todd Garvey and David H. Carpenter focuses on the ramifications that the *Noel Canning* decision might have on the President's authority to make recess appointment by providing a legal analysis of *Noel Canning* and the applicable case law that existed prior that decision. While sharing the general overview of the facts and legal reasoning necessary for understanding how *Noel Canning* might affect the NLRB and CFPB, this report does not duplicate the companion report's detailed constitutional analysis of the Recess Appointments Clause.

INTRODUCTION

On January 4, 2012, in the midst of a series of "pro forma" sessions, President Obama asserted his authority under the Recess Appointments Clause of the U.S. Constitution[1] and announced the appointments of Richard Cordray as Director of the Consumer Financial Protection Bureau (CFPB or Bureau) and Terrence F. Flynn, Sharon Block, and Richard F. Griffin, Jr. as Members of the National Labor Relations Board (NLRB or Board).[2] As a result of the controversial circumstances in which these appointments arose, numerous lawsuits have been initiated challenging the President's constitutional authority to make the appointments.[3]

On January 25, 2013, the U.S. Court of Appeals for the District of Columbia Circuit (D.C. Circuit) became the first court to evaluate the merits of these challenges. In *Noel Canning v. National Labor Relations Board*, the circuit court issued a broad decision invalidating the appointment of the three NLRB Board Members.[4] Although the decision directly applies only to the NLRB's authority to undertake the single action at issue in the case,[5] the legal reasoning, if adopted by other courts or affirmed by the Supreme Court, could significantly alter the relationship between the President and the Congress in the appointments context. It also would cast serious doubt not only upon an array of previous actions by the Board and its ability to function in the future, but also upon the validity of the President's appointment of Director Cordray; the validity of various actions already undertaken by the CFPB; and the authority of the CFPB to function going forward.[6]

THE APPOINTMENTS AND RECESS APPOINTMENTS CLAUSES

The U.S. Constitution allocates specific roles to both the President and the Senate in the appointment of government officials. The Constitution establishes two methods by which the President may make appointments. The Appointments Clause, which establishes the principal method of appointment, requires that the President

> *shall nominate, and by and with the Advice and Consent of the Senate, shall appoint* Ambassadors, other public Ministers and Consuls, Judges of the supreme Court, and all other *Officers of the United States* whose Appointments are not herein otherwise provided for, and which shall be established by Law; but *the Congress may by Law vest the Appointment of such inferior Officers*, as they think proper, *in the President alone, in the Court of Law, or in the Heads of Departments.*[7]

Thus, while the Appointments Clause authorizes the President to nominate principal officers of the United States,[8] a nominee cannot assume the powers of the office for which she has been nominated until confirmed by the Senate.[9]

In addition to this general provision, the Constitution also provides an alternative method of appointment that may be exercised only "during the Recess of the Senate." The Recess Appointments Clause (Clause) establishes that

> The President shall have Power to fill up all Vacancies that may happen during the Recess of the Senate, by granting Commissions which shall expire at the End of their next Session.[10]

The Recess Appointments Clause permits the President to make temporary appointments, without Senate approval, during periods in which the Senate is not in session.[11]

This constitutionally established appointment process, whether executed pursuant to the Appointments Clause or the Recess Appointments Clause, has often served as a source of political conflict between the President and Congress.[12] This tension between the branches is perhaps most acute when the Senate perceives the President as circumventing the Senate's constitutional "Advice and Consent" role by unilaterally appointing officials pursuant to the Recess Appointment Clause; or, conversely, when the President perceives the Senate as obstructing his duty to execute the laws by refusing to confirm nominees the President feels are qualified.

Absent a few generally established principles,[13] the Recess Appointments Clause is typically characterized as containing a number of inherent ambiguities. Most prominent among these lingering questions is the proper interpretation of the two phrases that form the very foundation of the Clause: "Vacancies that may happen during" and "the Recess of the Senate." With respect to the former phrase, must the vacancy *arise* during the recess in which the President exercises his appointment authority, or is it sufficient that the vacancy merely *exist* at the time the Senate is in recess and the appointment made? Regarding the latter, what is meant by "the Recess"? Specifically, is the President's recess appointment authority triggered only during intersession recesses (recesses *between* sessions of Congress) or may he also exercise his authority during intrasession recesses (recesses that occur *within* a session of Congress)?[14] Or to the contrary, is it the *duration*, rather than the form, of a recess that triggers the President's authority?

The executive branch and Congress have given some of these questions consideration in Attorneys General opinions[15] and committee reports, respectively.[16] The courts, however, have rarely engaged in any significant interpretive analysis of the Recess Appointments Clause. The Supreme Court, for example, has never considered when the President's appointment authority is triggered under the Clause, and prior to the D.C. Circuit's decision in *Noel Canning*, only three federal courts of appeals had engaged in such analyses. Those three decisions—*United States v. Allocco*,[17] *United States v. Woodley*,[18] and *Evans v. Stephens*[19]—arguably interpreted the Clause in a manner that imposed limited restrictions on the President's exercise of the recess appointment authority.[20] As is explained in *The Recess Appointment Power After Noel Canning v. NLRB: Constitutional Implications*, by Todd Garvey and David H. Carpenter, the D.C. Circuit's decision in *Noel Canning* contrasts significantly with *Allocco*, *Woodley*, and *Evans* regarding the ultimate scope of the President's authority under the Recess Appointments Clause.

THE JANUARY 4 APPOINTMENTS

The unique facts underlying President Obama's recess appointments of Cordray, Flynn, Block, and Griffin, Jr. have brought the inherent tensions of the appointments process into stark focus. President Obama formally nominated Cordray to be the first Director of the CFPB on July 18, 2011.[21] On October 6, 2011, the Senate Committee on Banking, Housing, and Urban Affairs approved Cordray's nomination for a full vote of the Senate.[22] However, on December 8, 2011, the Senate fell seven votes shy of the 60-vote threshold necessary to reach cloture and move to a vote on the nomination.[23]

The NLRB, an agency with certain powers to investigate and adjudicate unfair labor practices, consists of a board of up to five officials appointed by the President with the advice and consent of the Senate.[24] In 2011, the Board had only three Members—the minimum number of Members required for a quorum[25]—with one of the three scheduled to vacate his seat by the end of the first session of the 112th Congress. In an effort to prevent membership from dropping below the minimum quorum required for the Board to fully conduct business, President Obama nominated Flynn for a seat on the Board on January 5, 2011.[26] The President formally nominated Block and Griffin, Jr. for positions on the Board on December 15, 2011.[27] Two days later, the Senate adopted a unanimous consent agreement in which the body adjourned, but scheduled a series of "pro forma" sessions every three to four days to occur from December 20, 2011, until January 23, 2012. The unanimous consent agreement established that "no business" would be conducted during the pro forma sessions and that the second session of the 112th Congress would begin at 12:00 p.m. on January 3, 2012, as required by the Constitution.[28]

None of the four nominees were confirmed before the end of the first session of the 112th Congress. On January 4, the President, understanding the Senate to be in a recess, asserted his authority under the Recess Appointments

Clause and announced his appointment of Cordray, Block, Flynn, and Griffin, Jr.[29]

D.C. CIRCUIT: *NOEL CANNING V. NLRB*

Acting with its newly appointed Members, the NLRB issued an administrative decision against Noel Canning (a Pepsi distributor and bottler) in February 2012, ruling that the company had violated the National Labor Relations Act (NLRA) by failing to reduce to writing a collective bargaining agreement with a local Teamsters Union. Noel Canning challenged the NLRB's decision in the D.C. Circuit, claiming that three Members of the Board were invalidly appointed and that, as a result, the Board lacked a quorum to issue the decision.[30]

A unanimous three-judge panel held that the President's three recess appointments to the Board were constitutionally invalid. The opinion rested on two alternative justifications.

First, the court held that "the Recess," for purposes of the Clause, refers only to an intersession recess entered into at the end of a session of Congress.[31] To reach this holding, the D.C. Circuit placed significant importance on the Framers' choice of the phrase "the Recess," as opposed to "a recess," the plural "recesses" or the even broader "adjournment."[32] Looking to the "natural meaning of text as it would have been understood at the time of the ratification of the Constitution," the court concluded that the use of "the Recess," "points to the inescapable conclusion" that the Framers must have intended the Clause to mean something other than a "generic break in proceedings."[33]

Although the D.C. Circuit's holding that recess appointments may only be made during intersession recesses was sufficient to invalidate the President's appointments, a two-judge majority[34] also held that the President's recess appointments were invalid because the vacancies that were filled did not "happen during the Recess of the Senate."[35] The Court determined that the Clause authorizes the President to fill only those vacancies that "come into being" or "arise" during an intersession recess, rather than those that "happen to exist" during an intersession recess.[36] Moreover, the court held that the recess appointment must occur "during the same intersession recess when the vacancy for that office arose."[37] The court arrived at this construction because a plain reading of "that may Happen" could not properly be read to encompass all vacancies in existence, otherwise, the court argued, "the operative phrase ... would be wholly unnecessary."[38]

POTENTIAL IMPLICATIONS OF *NOEL CANNING* ON THE NLRB

The D.C. Circuit's actual order in *Noel Canning* vacated only the Board's administrative ruling that the bottling company had engaged in an unfair labor practice.[39] The decision did not invalidate any other Board actions, nor did the court issue an injunction preventing Members Block and Griffin, Jr. from taking any specific actions in the future.[40] Moreover, the decision only carries precedential value within the D.C. Circuit and in no way binds other federal courts outside of the circuit. Consequently, the opinion's immediate impact on the functioning of the Board may be limited as it only directly implicates the Board's action against Noel Canning within the D.C. Circuit. However, the court's determination that the Board Members were invalidly appointed may be widely applicable to legal challenges of other actions undertaken by the Board in which Flynn, Block, and Griffin, Jr. participated. For example, the more than 200 disputes on which the Board reportedly has ruled since the January 4, 2012 appointments likely would be called into question if the reasoning of *Noel Canning* is applied in future cases.[41]

The limitations on the reach of the appellate court's decision are reflected in the NLRB response to *Noel Canning*. Shortly after the decision, NLRB Chairman Mark Gaston Pearce announced that the NLRB "respectfully disagrees" with the D.C. Circuit's decision and noted that "similar questions have been raised in more than a dozen cases pending in other courts of appeals."[42] Given the decision's application to only "one specific case" and the Board's confidence that the "President's position in the matter will ultimately be upheld," Chairman Pearce asserted that the Board would "continue to perform our statutory duties and issue decisions."[43] As a result, it does not appear that the Board will interpret *Noel Canning* as mandating a stop to administrative proceedings. Indeed, in response to parties who have invoked *Noel Canning* in NLRB proceedings, the Board reportedly has concluded that these arguments "lack merit."[44]

Future Authority of the Board

Although the Chairman is correct that the D.C. Circuit decision applied only to the validity of the order issued against Noel Canning, the holding that Flynn, Block, and Griffin, Jr. were invalidly appointed is likely to be accorded significant precedential weight within the D.C. Circuit. Thus, within the D.C. Circuit's jurisdiction, the NLRB currently has only one validly appointed Member, and therefore lacks the statutorily defined minimum quorum necessary to fully function as determined by the Supreme Court in *New Process Steel, L.P. v. NLRB*.[45] As a result, until two additional Members are validly appointed, the D.C. Circuit likely will view the Board itself as without authority to take any action requiring a quorum of three Board Members.[46]

The D.C. Circuit's view of the Board's authority is unusually significant because section 10(f) of the NLRA allows final Board orders to be appealed by an aggrieved party to the U.S. Court of Appeals where the party resides or transacts business, where the unfair labor practice in question was alleged to have occurred, *or to the D.C. Circuit*.[47] Therefore, any party affected by a Board action—anywhere in the country—has the discretion to file a challenge to that action in the D.C. Circuit.[48] Once the challenge is before the D.C. Circuit, it is likely the court will follow the precedent established in *Noel Canning* and vacate the challenged Board action for lack of a quorum. Given these circumstances, the current Board may have difficulty enforcing its future actions.[49]

Past Actions of the Board

In addition to potentially restricting the Board's authority to act in the future, the reasoning underlying *Noel Canning* casts doubt on the legality of every substantive action taken by the Board during the tenures of Block, Flynn, and Griffin, Jr. Moreover, because the NLRA does not establish an explicit time limit on when Board orders may be appealed to a federal court of appeals,[50] legal uncertainty could surround any order issued in which a recess appointee appointed in conflict with the reasoning of *Noel Canning* participated in the decision and was necessary for meeting the Board's quorum requirement.[51] For example, there appear to have been periods in which the Board was composed of no more than two Senate-confirmed appointees dating back to at least the late 1980s.[52]

If parties were to challenge past actions of the Board, two legal doctrines might minimize the effect of a broader application of the *Noel Canning* holding: the de facto officer doctrine, which permits a court to validate an action of an official serving with apparent authority, to acknowledge that certain recess appointments were improper without invalidating all Board actions in which the appointees participated; and ratification by a properly constituted Board (i.e. a Board with at least three properly appointed Members). These two legal doctrines are discussed in greater detail below.

De Facto Officer Doctrine

The de facto officer doctrine "confers validity upon acts performed by a person acting under the color of official title even though it is later discovered that the legality of that person's appointment or election to office is deficient."[53] Thus, a reviewing court could invalidate the appointment of an officer, while limiting the remedies available to plaintiffs by applying the de facto officer doctrine to validate these past actions. The doctrine is intended to guard against "the chaos that would result from multiple and repetitious suits challenging every action taken by every official whose claim to office could be open to question, and seeks to protect the public by insuring the orderly functioning of the government despite technical defects in title to office."[54]

The courts have not established a clear test for when the de facto officer doctrine should be applied. However, the application of the doctrine appears to be shaped by two factors: the magnitude of constitutional or policy principles at stake and the timeliness of the challenge to the officer's appointment.[55]

In *Buckley v. Valeo*,[56] the Supreme Court held that the appointment of four Members of the Federal Election Commission (FEC) by Congress, rather than the President, violated the Appointments Clause.[57] The Court invalidated the appointments as unconstitutional, while also determining that

> the Commission's inability to exercise certain powers because of the method by which its members have been selected should not affect the validity of the Commission's administrative actions and determinations to this date. The past acts of the Commission are therefore accorded *de facto validity*.[58]

However, the Court in *United States v. Ryder* called into question the precedential value of *Buckley*'s "de facto validity" determination.[59] *Ryder* involved a challenge to a criminal conviction by the Coast Guard Court of Military Review because two of the three judges that decided the case were unconstitutionally appointed.[60] On appeal, the Court of Military Appeals held that the appointments were unconstitutional, but, citing *Buckley*, upheld the petitioner's conviction by applying the de facto officer doctrine. The Supreme Court reversed the Court of Military Appeals ruling. The *Ryder* Court reasoned that *Buckley* did not "explicitly rel[y] on the de facto officer doctrine ... ",[61] and instead "quite summarily held" that the FEC's prior actions were valid, de facto, while siding with the plaintiff on the constitutional questions raised and awarding his requested injunction and declaratory relief.[62] While the *Buckley* civil case may have been "thought to have implicitly applied a form of the de facto officer doctrine, we are not inclined to extend [the case] beyond [its] facts."[63] The Court also distinguished the facts in *Ryder* from those of three prior criminal cases in which de facto officer doctrine was applied by focusing on the timing of the appeal and the type of appointment defect in question:

> Unlike the defendants in *Ball*, *McDowell*, and *Ward*, petitioner [Ryder] raised his objection to the judges' titles before those very judges and prior to their action on his case. And his claim is based on the Appointments Clause ... rather than a misapplication of a statute providing for the assignment of already appointed judges to serve in other districts.[64]

The Court concluded that a "timely challenge to the constitutional validity" of an appointment warrants a "decision on the merits of the question and whatever relief may be appropriate if a violation indeed occurred."[65]

In the 2003 decision, *Nguyen v. United States*,[66] the Court ruled that the de facto officer doctrine should not be applied to uphold criminal convictions issued by a panel that included one improperly appointed judge, even though the challenge to the appointment was first made in a petition for *certiorari* to the Supreme Court, rather than before the panel that levied the conviction or on direct appeal.[67] To reach its conclusion, the Court analyzed precedents involving challenges to the appointments of judges. The Court explained that the de facto officer doctrine "[t]ypically" is applied in cases where a judicial appointment is challenged based on a "merely technical" statutory defect.[68] The Court has been more reticent to apply the doctrine in cases that hinge on more than mere technicalities, such as cases involving a statutory challenge "that 'embodies a strong policy concerning the proper administration of judicial business' even though the defect was not raised in a timely manner."[69] The Court illustrated the point through a quote from an 1893 decision:

> If the state made [the judge] incompetent to sit at the hearing, the decree in which he took part was unlawful, and perhaps absolutely void, and should certainly be set aside or quashed by any court having authority to review it by appeal, error or *certiorari*.[70]

Application of the De Facto Officer Doctrine to the NLRB

While it is difficult to predict how and when courts will apply the de facto officer doctrine, the cases indicate that the doctrine has been most commonly applied to validate the actions of officials whose appointments were infirm as a result of a *technical statutory* defect.[71] The doctrine is less likely to be applied where the defect in the officer's appointment involves (1) constitutional principles or fundamental policy issues,[72] especially when these objections are raised (2) timely and (3) directly.

A reviewing court likely would consider challenges to the January 4 appointments as raising significant constitutional issues, rather than technical statutory flaws. Consequently, the doctrine is unlikely to be applied to timely, direct challenges of the actions of these Board Members. There is, however, considerable uncertainty as to what challenges a court would consider to be both timely and direct. At the very least, it seems that the more time that has elapsed since the Board issued the order being challenged, the more likely it is that a reviewing court will consider validating the Board's past actions. For example, a court might apply the doctrine in cases contesting the actions of a Board from the 1980s that consisted of Members deemed to be appointed in conflict with the reasoning of *Noel Canning*.[73] Additionally, a court might be compelled to apply the doctrine where the party had previously appealed a Board order to a circuit court without raising an objection to the validity of the appointments, only to later collaterally attack a court's enforcement of that order on appointment grounds.

Ratification

Ratification, a legal doctrine derived from agency law, "occurs when a principal sanctions the prior actions of its agent."[74] A review of three court decisions illustrates how the doctrine may be applied by duly authorized governmental officers to affirm a past action performed by an officer subsequently determined to lack the authority to act, potentially without the need to redo the administrative procedures required by statute.

In *Federal Election Commission v. NRA Political Victory Fund*,[75] the FEC filed a petition for *writ of certiorari* to the Supreme Court without the approval of the Solicitor General, as was required by law. After the expiration of the statute of limitations to file the petition, the Solicitor provided approval for the FEC's petition.[76] The Supreme Court was left to "determine whether this 'after- the-fact' authorization relates back to the date of the FEC's unauthorized filing so as to make it timely."[77] According to the Court, "[t]he question is at least presumptively governed by ... the doctrine of ratification."[78] In order for the ratification to be valid, however, the ratifying party must have the legal authority to perform the act "*at the time the ratification was made*."[79] Because the Solicitor lacked the authority to file the writ on the day that he gave his approval, the Court held that he could not retroactively ratify the FEC's filing.[80]

In *Federal Election Commission v. Legi-Tech, Inc.*,[81] the D.C. Circuit was asked to affirm the lower court's dismissal of an enforcement action initiated by the FEC against Legi-Tech. While the Legi-Tech case was pending before the lower court, the D.C. Circuit ruled in a separate case that the FEC was "unconstitutionally constituted" because two of its non-voting, *ex officio* Members were appointed in contravention of the Appointments Clause.[82] In response, the FEC voted to reconstitute itself without the two invalid *ex officio* Members. The FEC began the administrative process of initiating the enforcement action against Legi-Tech while it was unconstitutionally composed.[83] After reconstituting itself without the invalid Members, the FEC continued its investigation against Legi-Tech and formally filed the action. Rather than starting the administrative process from scratch, the newly structured Commission ratified the past actions involving Legi-Tech.[84] The D.C. Circuit "assume[d] that no matter what course was followed— other than a dismissal with prejudice (which not even Legi-Tech dares request)—some effects of the unconstitutional structure of the FEC are to be presumed to have impacted on the action."[85] However, the court did not believe that the outcome would have changed significantly had the FEC started the entire process over.[86] Reversing the dismissal, the court concluded that "the better course is to take the FEC's post-reconstitution ratification of its prior decisions at face value and treat it as an adequate remedy for the [past] constitutional violation."[87]

Doolin Security Savings Bank v. Office of Thrift Supervision (OTS)[88] involved a fact pattern similar to that in *Legi-Tech*. OTS had determined to place a depository institution into receivership while Jonathan Fiechter was acting as the Director of OTS. Feichter had been appointed pursuant to questionable legal authority.[89] The enforcement action against the bank was completed under the leadership of the validly appointed Nicolas P. Retsinas.[90] Applying the reasoning of *NRA Political Victory Fund* and *Legi-Tech*, the court felt that "Retsinas made a detached and considered judgment in deciding the merits against the Bank." It also concluded that requiring the OTS to restart the administrative process would not have changed the outcome.[91] The court held that the enforcement action against the bank was valid because Retsinas "effectively ratified"[92] the enforcement proceedings initiated by Feichter "at a time when he could have initiated the charges himself."[93]

NLRB's Authority to Ratify Past Actions

In sum, agency actions taken by unconstitutionally appointed officers may be subsequently validated through the doctrine of ratification but only by a party that has the legal authority to perform the act at the time of the ratification. Thus, Board actions performed with the involvement of Block, Flynn, and Griffin, Jr. may be ratified by a Board consisting of at least three validly appointed Members. The *Legi-Tech* and *Doolin* decisions also indicate that the ratifying party, in this case a Board consisting of at least three validly appointed Members, may not be required to repeat all of the administrative steps performed by the unauthorized Members in order to validly ratify an action. Instead, the newly constituted Board could make it clear that they carefully and independently evaluated the prior proceedings and decided that the same outcomes were warranted.

POTENTIAL IMPLICATIONS OF *NOEL CANNING* ON THE CFPB

As previously mentioned, while the *Noel Canning* decision does not directly impact the CFPB, the legal reasoning of the case could be applied to the CFPB.[94] Challenges to the validity of Cordray's appointment currently are pending before multiple courts, including the U.S. District Court for the District of Columbia, where *Noel Canning* will hold significant precedential weight.[95] As a result, *Noel Canning* casts doubt not only over the validity of the President's appointment of Director Cordray, but also over various actions already undertaken by the CFPB and the authority of the CFPB to function going forward. The implications of a court ruling that Cordray's appointment was invalid would be complicated by the fact that no one prior to Cordray has served as CFPB Director and a provision of law appears to provide the Secretary of the Treasury the authority to exercise *some, but not all*, of the Director's powers until a Director is validly appointed. Specifically, section 1066(a) seems to authorize the Secretary to exercise those powers that were transferred to the Bureau from a number of other federal financial regulators, but not the Bureau's newly established authorities that were not held by other federal regulators prior to the enactment of the Consumer Financial Protection Act of 2010 (CFP Act).[96]

The Establishment of the Bureau and Director

The CFP Act[97] establishes the Bureau as an independent executive agency within the Federal Reserve System (FRS).[98] All of the Bureau's powers are concentrated within a single Director, who is to be appointed by the President, subject to the advice and consent of the Senate, to serve for a five-year term. The Director may only be removed by the President for "inefficiency, neglect of duty or malfeasance in office."[99] The Director may appoint a Deputy Director, who is authorized "to serve as acting Director in the absence or unavailability of the Director."[100] Additionally, the Director has authority to appoint and hire the employees necessary to carry out the duties of the Bureau[101] and "to delegate to any duly authorized employee, representative, or agent any power vested in the Bureau by law."[102]

The CFP Act empowers the Bureau through

1. the *transfer* of *existing* consumer protection powers from other federal regulators[103] ("transferred powers" or "transferred authorities"); and
2. *newly established* enhanced consumer protection authorities that were not explicitly provided by law to federal regulators prior to the Dodd-Frank Act's enactment ("newly established powers" or "newly established authorities").

The Bureau's transferred authorities include the power to issue rules to implement 19 federal consumer protection laws (the enumerated consumer laws) that, with one exception,[104] were enacted prior to the Dodd-Frank Act. They also include consumer compliance supervisory, enforcement, and rulemaking powers over banks, thrifts, and credit unions holding more than \$10 billion in deposits (larger depositories).[105]

The Bureau's newly established authorities largely consist of: enhanced, up-front supervisory and enforcement powers over covered non-depository financial institutions, such as payday and mortgage lenders;[106] new rulemaking powers, distinct from the rulemaking authorities provided under the enumerated consumer laws;[107] and certain limited consumer compliance enforcement and supervisory powers over "smaller depository institutions" (i.e., banks, thrifts, and credit unions with $10 billion or less in assets).[108]

Based on extent of the powers provided to the position, the CFPB Director arguably is an "Officer of the United States" who is exercising "significant"[109] governmental authorities.[110] If it were determined that, as a matter of law, Richard Cordray's appointment was invalid, then there would be no remaining "Officer[s] of the United States" appointed in accordance with the Constitution and CFP Act section 1011 to exercise the Director's powers. Additionally, if the Director position had never been validly filled, certain statutory avenues for temporarily filling the position would not apply to the CFPB. For instance, while the Bureau's Deputy Director is provided the authority to serve as acting director in the Director's absence, only the Director may appoint a Deputy Director.[111] If Cordray did not have the authority to exercise any Bureau powers, his appointment of a Deputy Director likely would be invalid.[112]

Consequently, in the absence of a congressional authorization to the contrary, it appears that no one may exercise the "significant authorities"[113] provided to the Bureau pursuant to the CFP Act until a Director is validly appointed in accordance with the Constitution. However, in order to prevent all of the CFPB's powers from remaining dormant until the indefinite time when a Director could be validly appointed, Congress appears to have empowered the Secretary of the Treasury to exercise the Bureau's transferred powers in accordance with section 1066(a).[114]

CFP Act Section 1066(a)

Presumably out of a recognition that it might take some time before a Director could be validly appointed, section 1066(a) of the CFP Act provides interim authority to the Secretary of the Treasury to exercise certain functions of the Bureau. Section 1066 is located within subtitle F of the CFP Act. The provisions of subtitle F transfer the relevant consumer financial protection functions and personnel from the five banking regulators, the Federal Trade Commission (FTC), and Department of Housing and Urban Development (HUD) to the CFPB. Section 1066(a) states,

> In General.—The Secretary [of the Treasury] is authorized to perform the functions of the Bureau *under this subtitle* until the Director of the Bureau is confirmed by the Senate in accordance with section 1011.[115]

Section 1066(a) is the only unexpired statutory provision in the CFP Act that provides substantial Bureau authorities to an officer or office other than the CFPB Director, the CFPB Deputy Director, or the Bureau itself.[116]

As is detailed below, the plain meaning of section 1066(a), its location within the structure of the CFP Act, the act's repeated distinction between transferred and newly established authorities, the legislative history of the provision, and the practical concerns that the provision seems to address point to the conclusion that the Secretary is authorized to exercise only the Bureau's *transferred powers*, which are effectuated pursuant to subtitle F, and only until a Bureau Director "is confirmed by the Senate.... "[117]

Plain Meaning, Location, and Structure

When required to interpret the meaning of a statute, courts typically will begin with an examination of the statutory text. Under the "plain meaning rule," judicial interpretation will begin and end with the text if its meaning is unambiguous.[118] Section 1066(a) expressly authorizes the Secretary's authority "to perform the functions of the Bureau *under this subtitle*." Section 1066 is located in subtitle F of the CFP Act. Additionally, no other provision of the CFP Act expressly authorizes the Secretary to perform substantive Bureau authorities.[119] As a result, CFP Act section 1066(a) seems to limit the Secretary's authorities to those provided to the Bureau under subtitle F.

In spite of this apparent plain meaning, at least one commentator has argued that the Secretary has the authority to exercise *all* of the Director's powers.[120] One problem with this argument is that an attempt to construe section 1066(a) as applying to all of the authorities provided under full CFP Act would render the phrase "under this subtitle" meaningless, which courts are hesitant to do.[121]

Additionally, had Congress intended to provide the Secretary *all* of the Bureau's authorities, it could have more clearly articulated that intent. One way this could have been accomplished is by substituting the word "title" for "subtitle," in order to reference the entire CFP Act (i.e., Title X of the Dodd-Frank Act), rather than just subtitle F (i.e., "Subtitle F—Transfer of Functions and Personnel; Transitional Provisions").[122] "Title" and "subtitle" are common terms used in legislative drafting, and the use of one over the other can dramatically alter statutory meaning. A reviewing court likely would presume that Congress intentionally chose the word "subtitle" rather than "title" unless there is "persuasive evidence" to the contrary.[123]

Furthermore, the CFP Act repeatedly distinguishes between authorities "transferred under subtitles F and H," "the enumerated consumer laws," and the other "provisions of this title," which arguably express a congressional understanding that each of these groups of powers is unique, and at times, must be treated differently from one another.[124] [Subtitle H, entitled "Conforming Amendments," effectuates the transfer of authorities provided in subtitle F by amending the enumerated consumer laws and other statutes.[125]] Notably, section 1027 of the CFP Act generally prohibits the Bureau from exercising its newly established supervisory, enforcement, and rulemaking authorities with respect to certain entities (e.g., real estate brokers), but those exemptions do not apply to the extent that the entities are "*otherwise subject to any enumerated consumer law or any law for which authorities are transferred under subtitle F or H*."[126]

Legislative History

A review of the legislative history of section 1066(a) suggests that several approaches were considered in five versions of three different bills.

First, section 166(a) of H.R. 3126 (111th Congress), which was marked-up by the House Committee on Financial Services (Financial Services Committee), used basically the same language as that of Dodd-Frank Act section 1066(a) that was signed into law, except that it accounted for the fact that, rather than being headed by a single director, the consumer agency under that particular proposal would have been run by a five-member board, each member of which was to "appointed by the President, by and with the advice and consent of the Senate."[127] H.R. 3126 (111th Congress) section 166(a) stated, in relevant part,

> In General—The Secretary is authorized to perform the functions of the Agency under this subtitle until 3 of the appointed Board members are confirmed by the Senate in accordance with section 112.

Ultimately, the bill that was ordered to be reported by the Financial Services Committee changed the leadership structure of the consumer agency to a single-directorship, but otherwise kept the relevant language providing the Secretary certain interim authorities intact.[128]

The House Committee on Energy and Commerce (Energy and Commerce Committee) also marked-up a discussion draft that ultimately was ordered to be reported as H.R. 3126 (111th Congress). The version that was ordered to be reported by the Energy and Commerce Committee would have structured the consumer agency as a five-member commission, but it did not amend the interim authority language of section 166(a).[129]

When this bill moved to the House Committee on Rules, it was merged into a comprehensive financial reform bill as H.R. 4173 (111th Congress). That bill's language initially passed the full House as section 4102 of H.R. 4173 (111th Congress). Section 4102 of that bill established the position of Director to head the proposed consumer agency. Section 4102 also provided that the individual *nominated* by the President to be the Director would serve as Acting Director of the agency.[130] The provision stated,

> The individual nominated pursuant to paragraph (1) [to be Director] shall serve as Acting Director with *full authorities granted to the Director under this title* until the Director is confirmed by the Senate. [131]

The bill that was discharged by unanimous consent from the Senate Committee on Banking, Housing, and Urban Affairs (Banking Committee) and passed the full Senate as H.R. 4173 (111th Congress) section 1066(a), in lieu of S. 3217 (111th Congress) section 1066(a), was identical to the language of the Dodd-Frank Act section 1066(a) that was signed into law.

In sum, section 4102 of the House-passed H.R. 4173 (111th Congress) would have provided an acting director the "*full* authorities" of the Director provided pursuant to the entire CFP Act ("under this *title*") until a Director could be validly appointed. Rather than follow this path, the Banking Committee began and ended with the language that ultimately was enacted into law as section 1066(a). While this legislative history does not conclusively prove congressional intent on the issue of interim authorities to exercise Bureau powers, it certainly does not provide a strong indication that Congress intended to provide the Secretary interim authorities beyond those described in section 1066(a)'s language.[132]

Practicalities of Section 1066

Finally, Congress had a practical justification for distinguishing between the transferred and newly established powers in context of the interim period before a Director was validly appointed—the regulatory scheme for the transferred powers had been in place for decades prior to the Dodd-Frank Act. The banking regulators have long held consumer compliance supervisory, enforcement, and rulemaking powers over large banks, thrifts, and credit unions. Many of the enumerated consumer laws also have been in place for significant periods of time.[133] Pursuant to the CFP Act, the transferred powers conveyed from the jurisdiction of the seven transferor agencies to the Bureau on a date certain—the designated transfer date.[134] Appointing officers subject to the advice and consent of the Senate is inherently uncertain. At the time of enactment, there was no way to guarantee that a Director could be in place by the designated transfer date. Had Congress not provided the Secretary (or some other valid officer) the authority to exercise those transferred powers, there would have been the possibility that no regulator had the authority to issue regulations under the enumerated consumer laws or to supervise the largest depository institutions in the country for compliance with consumer protection laws. For these reasons, Congress had compelling policy reasons to want to avoid such a regulatory gap. The policy justifications for ensuring that there were interim authorities to exercise the newly established powers are not as compelling because, before the Dodd-Frank Act, no such regulatory scheme existed.

In light of the plain language of section 1066, the structure of the CFP Act, the common uses of the terms within section 1066 in other places within the act, and the legislative history, coupled with the dearth of evidence to support an alternative interpretation, a reviewing court likely would determine that the Secretary of the Treasury is authorized to exercise the Bureau's transferred authorities until a CFPB Director is validly appointed, and that he has no authority to exercise the newly established powers.

Potential Impact on Past CFPB Actions

In light of the Secretary's authority to exercise the Bureau's transferred powers until a Director is validly appointed, a judicial determination that Richard Cordray's appointment was invalid could have a significant impact on past CFPB actions and the ability of the Bureau to act going forward.

For example, a court could conclude that every rulemaking and enforcement action conducted under the direction of Cordray was done without proper legal authority. However, unlike the statutory framework governing the NLRB which delegates authority to the Board alone, section 1066(a) appears to authorize the Secretary to exercise the CFPB's transferred powers until a Director is validly appointed. As is explained more specifically below, many of the substantive actions taken while Cordray was at the helm were exercises of transferred authorities that the Secretary could have authorized had he been serving as interim director pursuant to section 1066(a).[135] Consequently, the Secretary may be permitted to validate some of Bureau's past actions through the doctrine of ratification, which is discussed above.[136]

Rulemakings

The Bureau issued more than two dozen final rulemakings under Cordray's tenure as Director. Many of these rules were substantive issuances that potentially may have far-reaching impacts on consumer markets. Many also provide greater clarity and guidance to the industry on how to comply with statutory provisions that are, or soon will be, in effect. Questions about the enforceability and legal validity of these rules could cause widespread confusion among industry participants and could lead to market instability. To allay these concerns, the Secretary may have an incentive to ratify the rulemakings issued under Cordray pursuant to transferred powers.[137]

The majority of final regulations issued by the Bureau under Cordray's direction have been to implement one of the enumerated consumer laws.[138] The authority to issue rules under the enumerated consumer laws was transferred to the Bureau pursuant to subtitle F. Therefore, this authority would appear to fall within the Secretary's 1066(a) powers. For example, in February 2012, the CFPB issued final rules governing the provision of remittance transfers. These rules were amendments to Regulation E, which implements the EFTA, an enumerated consumer law.[139] Additionally, in January 2013, the Bureau issued a series of mortgage servicing and mortgage origination final regulations largely to implement provisions of Dodd-Frank Act, Title XIV. Each of these mortgage-related rulemakings amended either Regulation Z or Regulation X, which implement the enumerated consumer laws the Truth in Lending Act[140] and the Real Estate Settlement Procedures Act,[141] respectively.[142]

The Bureau also issued two rules to define certain credit reporting agencies[143] and certain debt collectors[144] as nondepository financial institutions that would be subject to the CFPB's supervision pursuant to CFP Act section 1024.[145] Section 1024 is a newly established power that likely is outside the scope of the Secretary's authority under section 1066(a). Therefore, the Secretary would not have the authority to ratify these rulemakings, and they probably could not be legally enforced by the Bureau until a Director is validly appointed. These appear to be the only substantive rulemakings issued pursuant to newly established authorities that seem to be outside of the scope of the Secretary's 1066(a) powers.[146]

Enforcement Actions

From the time of Cordray's appointment until the D.C. Circuit's *Noel Canning* decision, the CFPB had only entered into five formal enforcement actions.[147] Each of these actions was against a larger depository[148] and took the form of a consent order, to which the depositories voluntarily agreed. Pursuant to section 1066(a), the Secretary has the authority to supervise and engage in enforcement actions with each of the parties to these consent orders. However, each of the orders relied, at least in part, on the CFPB's newly established authority to prohibit unfair, deceptive, or abusive practices (UDAP).[149] Without the newly established UDAP arrow in its enforcement quiver, the CFPB, under the Secretary's direction, may not have the negotiating leverage to reach the same terms, if there is an attempt to ratify the orders with the consent of the parties.

Unlike the broadly applicable rulemakings, the terms of the five enforcement actions only apply to the small number of financial institutions that are parties to the agreements. For this reason, the Bureau may not have a strong incentive to proactively ratify the consent orders (or enter into new ones). Instead, the Bureau might choose to wait for the named parties to seek judicial relief from the terms of the orders. Since all of the named parties are larger depositories that will remain subject to the Bureau's regulatory jurisdiction under the direction of the Secretary, they may have practical reasons for not wanting to litigate the matter. Additionally, each of these parties failed to challenge the constitutionality of Cordray's appointment, and thus the authority to enter the enforcement actions, when the orders were being negotiated. Under these circumstances, a reviewing court might be more likely to apply the de facto officer doctrine to uphold the validity of these consent orders due to the belatedness of any future challenge.

End Notes

[1] U.S. Const. art. II, §2, cl. 3.

[2] *President Obama Announces Recess Appointments to Key Administration Posts*, White House, Press Release, Jan. 4, 2012, available at http://www.whitehouse.gov/the-press-office/2012/01/04/president-obama-announces-recess- appointments-key-administration-posts.

[3] See Lyle Denniston, *Spreading challenge to appointment power (UPDATED)*, SCOTUSblog, Jan. 28, 2013, available at http://www.scotusblog.com/2013/01/spreading-challenge-to-appointment-power/; Complaint, State Nat'l Bank of Big Spring v. Geithner, Case No. 1:12-cv-01032 (D.C. Sept. 20, 2012), available at http://newsandinsight. thomsonreuters.com/ uploadedFiles/Reuters_Content/2012/09_-_September/statenationvcfpb—amended complaint.pdf; Opposition to Receiver's Second Request for Payment, Consumer Fin. Prot. Bureau v. Gordon, Case No. CV12-6147-RSWL(MRWx), (C.D.Cal. July 18, 2012), available at http://www.cfpbmonitor. com/files/2013/ 02/CGCFPB-Opp-Rec-Req-2.pdf.

[4] No. 12-115 (D.C. Cir., Jan. 25, 2013) (hereinafter *Noel Canning*) available at http://www. cadc.uscourts.gov/internet/opinions.nsf/D13E4C2A7B33B57A85257AFE00556B29/$file/1 2-1115-1417096.pdf.

[5] The decision only carries precedential value within the D.C. Circuit and in no way binds other federal courts outside of the circuit. In making future recess appointments, the Obama Administration—which has stated that it disagrees with the Noel Canning decision—may not feel bound by the restrictions established by the circuit court until the Supreme Court takes a position on the issue. However, a plaintiff challenging a future recess appointment to a position located within the District of Columbia would likely have the choice of filing that lawsuit in the D.C. Circuit where *Noel Canning* would be accorded significant precedential weight.

[6] Taken to its logical limits, the reasoning of the opinion could create uncertainty as to the validity of hundreds of other recess appointments made across the government in recent years. Consideration of these appointments is beyond the scope of this report.

[7] U.S. Const. art. II, §2, cl. 2 (emphasis added).

[8] The Supreme Court has distinguished "principal officers," who must be appointed by the President with the advice and consent of the Senate, from inferior officers, whose appointment Congress may vest solely in the President, the judiciary, or a head of a department. U.S. Const. art. II, §2, cl. 2. The differences between principal and inferior officers is discussed in the "The Establishment of the Bureau and Director" section below.

[9] Once confirmed by the Senate, an officer is not formally appointed until his commission is signed by the President.

[10] U.S. Const. art. II, §2, cl. 3.

[11] CRS Report RL33009, *Recess Appointments: A Legal Overview*, by Vivian S. Chu.

[12] *Id.* at 2 (citing numerous examples of contentious recess appointments).

[13] CRS Report R43030, *The Recess Appointment Power After Noel Canning v. NLRB: Constitutional Implications*, by Todd Garvey and David H. Carpenter, pp. 3-4.

[14] It should be noted that prior to the Civil War intrasession recesses were relatively uncommon as Congress generally met for relatively short sessions followed by long intersession recesses of six to nine months.

[15] For example, aspects of the recess appointments power were considered as early as 1792, and there were at least 19 formal Attorneys General opinions in the 19th century on recess appointments, the earliest written in 1823. See CRS Report RL33009, *Recess Appointments: A Legal Overview*, by Vivian S. Chu.

[16] See, e.g. S.Rpt. No. 58-4389 at 2 (1905) ("[Recess] means, in our judgment, in this connection the period of time when the Senate is *not sitting in regular or extraordinary session as a branch of the Congress* ... ; when its members owe no duty of attendance; when its Chamber is empty; when, because of its absence, it can not [*sic*] receive communications from the President or participate as a body in making appointments.") (emphasis in original).

[17] 305 F.2d 704 (2nd Cir. 1962).

[18] 751 F.2d 1008 (9th Cir. 1985).

[19] 387 F.3d 1220 (11th Cir. 2004).

[20] All three cases arose in the context of judicial appointments, and all three courts also held that the Recess Appointments Clause authorized the President to fill judicial vacancies.

[21] 157 CONG. REC. S4646 (daily ed. July 18, 2011). Title X of the Dodd-Frank Wall Street Reform and Consumer Protection Act (Dodd-Frank Act) established the CFPB and provided the independent agency with rulemaking, enforcement, and supervisory powers over many consumer financial products and services, as well as the entities that provide them.

[22] *Johnson Statement on Committee Approval of Richard Cordray's Nomination to Lead the CFPB*, S. Comm. on Banking, Hous., and Urban Affairs, Press Release, Oct. 6, 2011, available at http://shelby.senate.gov/public/index.cfm/ newsreleases?ContentRecord_id=893bc8b0-2e73-4555-8441-d51e0ccd1d17.

[23] 157 CONG. REC. S8429 (daily ed. Dec. 8, 2011).

[24] 29 U.S.C. §153.

[25] In 2010, the Supreme Court ruled that the NLRA prevents the NLRB from exercising rulemaking powers without having three or more acting Members. New Process Steel v. Nat'l Labor Relations Bd., 130 S. Ct. 2635 (2010).

[26] 157 CONG. REC. S68 (daily ed. Jan. 5, 2011).

[27] 157 CONG. REC. S8691 (daily ed. Dec. 15, 2011). President Obama had nominated Craig Becker on January 26, 2011 to retain the seat on the Board that he had previously held by recess appointment. That nomination was withdrawn on December 15, 2011. *Id.*

[28] 157 CONG. REC. S883-S8784 (daily ed. Dec. 17, 2011). The unanimous consent agreement stated that the Senate would "adjourn and convene for pro forma sessions only, with no business conducted" on December 20, 23, 27, and 30; that the second session of the 112th Congress would convene on January 3 at noon "for a pro forma session only, with no business conducted;" and that the Senate would then convene for pro forma sessions "with no business conducted" on January 6, 10, 13, 17, and 20, 2012.

[29] *President Obama Announces Recess Appointments to Key Administration Posts*, White House, Press Release, Jan. 4, 2012, available at http://www.whitehouse.gov/the-press-office/2012/01/04/president-obama-announces-recess- appointments-key-administration-posts. The appointments occurred in the time between pro forma sessions on January 3 and January 6, 2012.

[30] Noel Canning v. Nat'l Labor Relations Bd., No. 12-1115 (D.C. Cir. Jan. 25, 2013).

[31] *Id.* at 16-30.

[32] *Noel Canning,* No. 12-115, at 16-18.

[33] *Id.* at 17.

[34] Noting that the "intersession recess" holding was sufficient to invalidate the appointments, Judge Griffith did not join the court's holding that a vacancy also must arise during "the Recess." *Id.* at 47 (Griffith, J. concurring).

[35] *Id.* at 30-44. The court began its analysis "by looking at the natural meaning of the text as it would have been understood at the time of the ratification of the Constitution." *Id.* at 30-31.

[36] *Id.* at 30-31. ("Upon a simple reading of the language itself, we conclude that the word 'happen' could not logically have encompassed any vacancies that happened to exist during 'the Recess.'").

[37] *Id.* at 43-44.

[38] *Id.* at 31. The court acknowledged that this interpretation directly conflicted with the decisions in *Allocco*, *Woodley*, and *Evans*, but criticized those decisions for relying on modern dictionaries to define "happen," rather than contemporary 18th century dictionaries that would define the term as understood during the time of ratification. *Id.* at 35-36.

[39] Although the order does not appear to question either the authority of NLRB regional offices or NLRB Administrative Law Judges (ALJs) to continue to function pursuant to NLRA delegations, any ALJ or Regional Director appointed by the Board after the January 4 appointments may be subject to challenge under the theory that the Board lacked authority to make the appointment.

[40] Flynn resigned as Member of the Board on July 24, 2012. *National Labor Relations Board Member Terrence Flynn Resigns*, Press Release, Nat'l Labor Relations Bd., May 27, 2012.

[41] Any extension of the holding in *Noel Canning* would need to be achieved through future litigation.

[42] *Statement by Chairman Pearce on Recess Appointment Ruling*, NLRB News Release Jan. 25, 2013. The NLRB has stated that it intends to file a petition for certiorari with the Supreme Court by Apr. 25, 2013. *NLRB To Seek Supreme Court Review in Noel Canning v. NLRB*, NLRB News Release March 12, 2013.

[43] *Id.*

[44] Counsel for the Acting General Counsel's Reply Brief to Respondent's Answering Brief, 24 Hour Fitness USA, Inc. v. Nat'l Labor Relations Bd., Case No. 20-CA-35419, Mar. 7, 2013 ("It is not appropriate for the Board to suspend its activities in response to a claim that Presidential appointments to the Board are not valid. Although, Respondent correctly points

out that the D.C. Circuit has recently held that the President's appointments to the Board were not valid, the Board has publicly stated that it disagrees with that decision. In addition, it should be noted that in *Noel Canning* the D.C. Circuit Court itself noted that its conclusions concerning the Presidential Appointments had been rejected by the other circuit courts to address the issues. Moreover, even in the absence of a circuit conflict, it has been the Board's longstanding practice not to acquiesce in adverse decisions by individual courts of appeals in subsequent proceedings involving different parties.") (internal citations omitted).

[45] 130 S.Ct. 2635, 2640 (2010) (interpreting 29 U.S.C. §153(b) to require "three participating members 'at all times' for the Board to act.").

[46] *Id.* at 9-10, n. 4 ("The Board may not, of course, itself take any action absent sufficient membership to muster a quorum (three), and in that sense a quorum requirement establishes a minimum membership level."). The Supreme Court left open the possibility that non-Board members, such as regional directors and the Board's general counsel, may exercise certain powers provided by the NLRA in absence of a quorum on the Board. *Id.* ("Our conclusion that the delegee group ceases to exist once there are no longer three Board members to constitute the group does not cast doubt on the prior delegations of authority to nongroup members, such as the regional directors or the general counsel. The latter implicates a separate question that our decision does not address.").

[47] 29 U.S.C. §160(f) (emphasis added).

[48] In making future recess appointments, the Obama Administration—which has stated that it disagrees with the Noel Canning decision—may not feel bound by the restrictions established by the circuit court until the Supreme Court takes a position on the issue. However, a plaintiff challenging a future recess appointment to a position located within the District of Columbia would likely have the choice of filing that lawsuit in the D.C. Circuit where *Noel Canning* would be accorded significant precedential weight.

[49] The NLRB orders generally are not self-executing, but the Board is authorized to seek an enforcement order from a U.S. Circuit Court of Appeals. 29 U.S.C. §160(e). Unless overturned by the Supreme Court, the *Noel Canning* holding also likely will apply to cases challenging Board actions that are currently pending before the D.C. Circuit. However, at this time, the court has held most of these cases in abeyance "pending further order of the court." See, e.g., Order No. 12-5250, Chamber of Commerce of the United States v. Nat'l Labor Relations Bd., 1:11-cv-02262-JEB, (D.C. Cir., Feb. 19, 2013), available at http://www.chamberlitigation. com/sites/default/files/cases/files/2011/ D.C.%20Circuit%20Order%20removing%20 from%20calendar%20and%20holding%20in%20abeyance.pdf. Claims that are currently pending in other circuit courts may have more difficulty taking advantage of the *Noel Canning* holding. See CRS Legal Sidebar Post WSLG411, Noel Canning and the National Labor Relations Board, by Jon O. Shimabukuro. Other circuit courts would not be bound by the D.C. Circuit's *Noel Canning* decision, but they may be influenced by it.

[50] Buchannan v. Nat'l Labor Relations Bd., 597 F.2d 388, 392 (4th Cir. 1979) ("This is a clear signal that Congress intended a 'no time limit' under the National Labor Relations Act for petitions to courts of appeals."); Griffith Co. v. Nat'l Labor Relations Bd., 545 F.2d 1194 (9th Cir. 1976); Kovach v. Nat'l Labor Relations Bd., 229 F.2d 138 (7th Cir. 1956).

[51] See, e.g., Citation of Supplemental Authorities Pursuant to Rule 28(j) of the Federal Rules of Appellate Procedure, D.R. Horton, Inc. v. Nat'l Labor Relations Bd. Case No. 12-60031 (5th Cir., Jan. 29, 2013), available at http://amlawdaily.typepad.com/hortoncanningletter.pdf (arguing that the appointment of Member David Becker was invalid under the reasoning of *Noel Canning*, and, without Becker, the NRLB did not have sufficient quorum at the time that it issued an order against petitioner; therefore, the order also is invalid).

[52] See *Members of the NLRB since 1935*, available at http://www.nlrb.gov/members-nlrb-1935. Questions regarding the impact of *Noel Canning* on the validity of other recess appointees are beyond the scope of this report.

[53] Ryder v. United States, 515 U.S. 177, 180 (1995) (quoting Norton v. Shelby County, 118 U.S. 425, 440 (1886)).

[54] *Ryder*, 515 U.S. at 180-81 (quoting 63A, Am Jur. 2d., Public Officers and Employees §578, pp. 1080-81 (1984)).

[55] See *Ryder*, 515 U.S. at 180-83; Ronald M. Levin, *"Vacation" At Sea: Judicial Remedies and Equitable Discretion in Administrative Law*, 53 Duke L. J. 293, 326-29 (2003).

[56] 424 U.S. 1 (1976).

[57] *Buckley*, 424 U.S. at 140-42. See *Ryder*, 515 U.S. at 183 ("Neither *Buckley* nor *Connor* explicitly relied on the de facto officer doctrine, though the result reached in each case validated the past acts of public officials.").

[58] *Buckley*, 424 U.S. at 142 (emphasis added). The *Buckley* Court issued a temporary stay in order to provide "Congress an opportunity to reconstitute the Commission ..., allowing the present Commission in the interim to function de facto in accordance with the substantive provisions of the Act." *Id.*

[59] *Ryder*, 515 U.S. at 184 ("To the extent that these civil cases [*Buckley* and *Connor*] may be thought to have implicitly applied a form of the de facto officer doctrine, we are not inclined to extend them beyond their facts.").

[60] The two judges, who were determined to be inferior officers, were appointed by the General Counsel of the Department of Transportation, rather than by the President, a department head, or a court, as is required by the Appointments Clause. *Ryder*, 515 U.S. at 179-80.

[61] *Ryder*, 515 U.S. at 183.

[62] *Id.* (internal quotations omitted).

[63] *Id.* at 184.

[64] *Id.* at 181-82 (internal citations omitted) (citing McDowell v. United States, 159 U.S. 596, 598-601 (1895) (applying the de facto officer doctrine because McDowell failed to challenge the validity of a judge's appointment until after indictment and trial and because his challenge "presents a mere matter of statutory construction ... It involves no trespass upon the executive power of appointment."); Ball v. United States, 140 U.S. 118, 128-29 (1891) (applying the de facto officer doctrine to deny requested relief of a criminal defendant who did not challenge the validity of his sentencing judge's appointment until after his sentencing)).

[65] *Ryder*, 515 U.S. at 182-83. See also Nguyen v. United States, 539 U.S. 69, 78 (2003) ("By contrast, we have agreed to correct, at least on direct review, violations of a statutory provisions that 'embodies a strong policy concerning the proper administration of judicial business' even though the defect was not raised in a timely manner."); Office of Thrift Supervision v. Paul, 985 F. Supp. 1465, 1475 (S.D. Fla. 1997) ("*Ryder* does provide an exception to the *de facto* officer doctrine, specifically when 'one makes a timely challenge to the constitutional validity of the appointment of an officer who adjudicates his case.'"); In re Fichner, 144 N.J. 459, 471 (N.J. 1996) ("In *Ryder*, ... the Supreme Court permitted a constitutional challenge to the composition of the Board of Military Review but only because the issue had been raised in a direct challenge while the case was pending before that Board.... ").

[66] 539 U.S. 69 (2003).

[67] *Id.* at 73 and 80.

[68] *Id.* at 77 (2003) (quoting Glidden Co. v. Zdanok, 370 U.S. 530, 535 (1962) (plurality)) ("In *McDowell v. United States*, for example, the Court declined to notice alleged irregularities in a Circuit Judge's designation for temporary service in another district ... [because] the judge whose assignment had been questioned was otherwise qualified to serve, because he was a judge of the United States District Court, having all powers attached to such office, and because the Circuit Judge was otherwise empowered to designate him.") (internal citations and quotations omitted). See also *Ryder*, 515 U.S. at 181-82.

[69] *Nguyen*, 539 U.S. at 78 (quoting *Glidden*, 370 U.S. at 536). See also *Ryder*, 515 U.S. at 182-83.

[70] *Nguyen*, 539 U.S. at 78 (quoting American Constr. Co. v. Jacksonville, T. & K. W. R. Co., 148 U.S. 372, 387 (1893)).

[71] For an example of a "technical statutory defect" recognized by a court, see *supra* n. 68.

[72] *Id.* at 80.

[73] As previously mentioned, the NLRA does not provide a statute of limitations for appeals of Board orders. See *supra* n. 50.

[74] Doolin Sec. Sav. Bank v. Office of Thrift Supervision, 139 F.3d 203 (D.C. Cir. 1998) (citing Restatement (Second) of Agency §82 (1958)).

[75] 513 U.S. 88 (1994).

[76] *Id.* at 98.

[77] *Id.*

[78] *Id.*

[79] *Id.* (emphasis original) (quoting Cook v. Tullis, 18 Wall. 332, 338 (1874)).

[80] *Id.* at 98-99.

[81] 75 F.3d 704 (D.C. Cir. 1996).

[82] *Id.* at 706 (citing Federal Election Comm'n v. NRA Political Victory Fund, 6 F.3d 821 (D.C. Cir. 1993)).

[83] *Id.* at 706.

[84] *Id.* at 707.

[85] *Id.* at 708.

[86] *Id.* at 708-09.

[87] *Id.* at 709.

[88] 139 F.3d 203 (D.C. Cir. 1998).

[89] *Id.* at 204. The court did not need to reach a conclusion regarding the validity of Feichter's appointment because it held that the his successor was validly appointed and ratified Feichter's actions. *Id.* at 214 ("Because we hold that Retsinas effectively ratified the Notice of Charges signed by Fiechter at a time when he could have initiated the charges himself, we do not decide whether Fiechter lawfully occupied the position of Director.").

[90] *Id.*

[91] *Id.* at 213-14.

[92] The court found the ratification was effective in spite of the fact that Retsinas never explicitly "invoke[d] the term." *Id.* at 213-14. The court explained: "Retsinas issued the order after reviewing the evidence, explaining his reasons, and concluding that the Bank had violated the law. This had the legal consequence of ratifying Fiechter's [actions] ... even though Retsinas did not say as much." *Id.* at 214, n. 11 (internal citations omitted).

[93] *Id.* at 212-14. As a result, the court did not have to "decide whether Feichter lawfully occupied the position of Director." *Id.* at 214.

[94] In fact, the *Noel Canning* court noted that "early interpreters [] understood that the Clause only applied to vacancies where the office had previously been occupied, as opposed to vacancies that existed because the office had been newly created." *Noel Canning*, at 34-35.

[95] See, e.g., Complaint, State Nat'l Bank of Big Spring v. Geithner, Case No. 1:12-cv-01032 (D.C. Sept. 20, 2012), available at http://newsandinsight.thomsonreuters.com/uploadedFiles/Reuters_Content/2012/09_-_September/ statenationvcfpb—amendedcomplaint.pdf; Opposition to Receiver's Second Request for Payment, Consumer Fin. Prot. Bureau v. Gordon, Case No. CV12-6147-RSWL(MRWx), (C.D.Cal. July 18, 2012), available at http://www.cfpbmonitor.com/files/2013/02/CGCFPB-Opp-Rec-Req-2.pdf.

[96] For a more in-depth legal analysis of the CFP Act, see CRS Report R42572, *The Consumer Financial Protection Bureau (CFPB): A Legal Analysis*, by David H. Carpenter.

[97] The CFP Act is enacted as Title X of the Dodd-Frank Wall Street Reform and Consumer Protection Act (Dodd-Frank Act), P.L. 111-203.

[98] Dodd-Frank Act §1011; 12 U.S.C. §5491. Although the Bureau is housed within the FRS, it has considerable independence from the Board of Governors of the Federal Reserve System (FRB).

[99] Dodd-Frank Act §1011, 12 U.S.C. §5491.

[100] Dodd-Frank Act §1011, 12 U.S.C. §5491.

[101] Dodd-Frank Act §1013, 12 U.S.C. §5493.

[102] Dodd-Frank Act §1012, 12 U.S.C. §5492.

[103] The seven "transferor agencies" are the five federal banking regulators—the Office of the Comptroller of the Currency (OCC); the FRB; the Federal Deposit Insurance Corporation (FDIC); the National Credit Union Administration (NCUA); and OTS—as well as the Federal Trade Commission (FTC), and the Department of Housing and Urban Development (HUD).

[104] The Bureau acquired rulemaking authority pursuant to most provisions of the Mortgage Reform and Anti-Predatory Lending Act, which was enacted as Title XIV of the Dodd-Frank Act. Dodd-Frank Act §1400. The majority of these provisions are enacted as amendments to TILA or RESPA.

[105] Dodd-Frank Act §§1061-1067, 12 U.S.C. §§5581-5587. More specifically, the transferred authorities include

- "all authority to prescribe rules or issue orders or guidelines pursuant to any Federal consumer financial law," including the rulemaking authority under the 18 enumerated consumer laws, held by the HUD, FRB, OCC, OTS, FDIC, and NCUA;
- certain consumer compliance examination and other supervisory authorities over larger depositories;
- primary enforcement authority of consumer financial laws and regulations over larger depositories;
- subject to certain limitations, the FTC's authority "to prescribe rules, issue guidelines, or conduct a study or issue a report mandated under [the enumerated consumer laws] ... ";
- the authority to coordinate a process by which certain employees of all of the transferor agencies other than the FTC are identified to be transferred to the CFPB, as necessary to perform the transferred authorities. Dodd-Frank Act §1061, 12 U.S.C. §5581.

[106] Dodd-Frank Act §1024, 12 U.S.C. §5514.

[107] See, e.g., Dodd-Frank Act §§1022, 1031-1036, 12 U.S.C. §§5512, 5531-36.

[108] Dodd-Frank Act §1026(a), 12 U.S.C. §5516. The banking regulators retained both safety and soundness and primary consumer compliance authorities over smaller depositories.

[109] Quoting *Buckley*, 424 U.S. at 126, n. 162 ("'Officers of the United States' does not include all employees of the United States.... Employees are lesser functionaries subordinate to the officers of the United States.") ("Officers of the United States" refers to "any appointee exercising significant authority pursuant to the laws of the United States."). An individual "exercising significant authority" of the United States generally is either a principal or inferior officer, who must be appointed in accordance with Appointments Clause or Recess Appointments Clause. *Id.* See also Edmond v. United States, 520 U.S. 651, 662 (1997) ("The exercise of 'significant authority pursuant to the laws of the United States' marks, not the line between principal and inferior officer for Appointments Clause purposes, but rather, as we said in *Buckley*, the line between officer and non-officer."). See also United States v. Germaine, 99 U.S. 508, 511-12 (1878) (an officer "embraces the ideas of tenure, duration, emolument, and duties, and that the latter [are] continuing and permanent, not occasional or temporary.")

[110] U.S. Const. art. II, §2, cl. 2. The fact that the Director may only be removed for cause and only by the President, the fact that the Director is not subject to direct oversight or supervision of any other executive officer, the broad scope of the Director's powers, and the permanent tenure of the office of the Director all strongly indicate that the Director is, in fact, a *principal* officer of the United States. Regardless of the type of officer, Congress, through

the CFP Act, requires that the Director be appointed by the President and confirmed by the Senate. Dodd-Frank Act §1011, 12 U.S.C. §5491.

[111] Dodd-Frank Act §1011, 12 U.S.C. §5491.

[112] Additionally, the Vacancies Reform Act (VRA), a statutory alternative to filling some advice and consent positions, would not be applicable to the CFPB Director position. Under the VRA, a "vacancy" arises when the relevant officer "dies, resigns, or is otherwise unable to perform the functions and duties of the office." 5 U.S.C. §3345(a). If Cordray's appointment was invalid, the Director position would be vacant because it had never been filled, rather than for one of the VRA's triggering events—death, resignation, or inability to perform.

[113] Quoting *Buckley*, 424 U.S. at 126, n. 162.

[114] *Buckley*, 424 U.S. at 162. Before statutory authority may be exercised, it must be both effective and a government actor (i.e., principal officer, inferior officer, or non-officer employee) must be authorized to wield it. The Supreme Court's interpretation of the NLRA in *New Process Steel* provides a clear example of this in practice. Although the NLRB's powers under the NLRA clearly had gone into effect, the Board lacked the authority to exercise those powers for want of a quorum. *New Process Steel*, 130 S.Ct. at 2644-45.

[115] Dodd-Frank Act §1066(a), 12 U.S.C. §5586(a) (emphasis added).

[116] Three other CFP Act provisions provided the Secretary authority related to the Bureau; however, those authorities terminated on July 21, 2011, the designated transfer date. Dodd-Frank Act §1062, 12 U.S.C. §5582 (authority to establish the designated transfer date, in consultation with other regulators); Dodd-Frank Act §1017(a)(3), 12 U.S.C. §5497(a)(3) (authority to request funds from the FRB until the designated transfer date); Dodd-Frank Act §1066(b), 12 U.S.C. §5586(b) (authority for the Treasury Department to "provide administrative services necessary to support the Bureau.... "). Additionally, until July 21, 2014, the President has the authority to settle disputes among the Bureau and the transferor agencies regarding the transfer of functions and personnel in accordance with subtitle F. Dodd-Frank Act §1064(a)(8), 12 U.S.C. 5584(a)(8).

[117] As is explained in detail in CRS Report R42323, *President Obama's January 4, 2012, Recess Appointments: Legal Issues*, by David H. Carpenter et al., at 30-36, it is unlikely that a reviewing court would interpret section 1066(a) as restricting a validly appointed recess appointee, as compared to a Senate-confirmed appointee, from exercising the full authorities of the Director position.

[118] CRS Report 97-589, *Statutory Interpretation: General Principles and Recent Trends*, by Larry M. Eig.

[119] See *supra* n. 116.

[120] See, e.g., *Hurdle for Challengers to CFPB Recess Appointment: Consumer Bureau Had Full Power With or Without a Director*, Nat'l Consumer Law Ctr., Feb. 2012, available at http://www.nclc.org/images/pdf/regulatory_reform/issue- brief-cfpb-interim-powers.pdf (arguing that section 1066(a) provides the Secretary the authority to exercise *all* Bureau powers until a Director is validly appointed). But see *Review of CFPB Implementation Planning Activities*, Offices of Inspector General, Bd. of Governors of the Fed. Reserve Sys. and Bureau of Consumer Fin. Prot. and Dept. of the Treasury, at 2-4, July 15, 2011, available at http://www.federalreserve.gov/oig/files/ OIG_2011_Review_of_CFPB_ Implementation_Planning_Activities.pdf.

[121] See, e.g., *New Process Steel,* 130 S.Ct. at 2640 ("See Duncan v. Walker, 533 U. S. 167, 174 (2001) (declining to adopt a 'construction of the statute, [that] would render [a term] insignificant'); Market Co. v. Hoffman, 101 U. S. 112, 115-116 (1879) ('[A] statute ought, upon the whole, to be so construed that, if it can be prevented, no clause, sentence, or word shall be ... insignificant' (internal quotation marks omitted)."). See also CRS Report 97-589, *Statutory Interpretation: General Principles and Recent Trends*, by Larry M. Eig.

[122] See, e.g., *New Process Steel*, 130 S.Ct. at 2641 ("Second, and relatedly, if Congress had intended to authorize two members alone to act for the Board on an ongoing basis, it could

have said so in straightforward language."). See also CRS Report 97-589, *Statutory Interpretation: General Principles and Recent Trends*, by Larry M. Eig, at 16.

[123] See, e.g., Boston Sand & Gravel Co. v. United States, 278 U.S. 41, 48 (1928) (holding that federal statute does not make government liable for interest in a collision with a U.S. naval ship) ("It is said that when the meaning of language is plain we are not to resort to evidence in order to raise doubts. That is rather an axiom of experience than a rule of law, and does not preclude consideration of persuasive evidence if it exists.... "). See CRS Report 97-589, *Statutory Interpretation: General Principles and Recent Trends*, by Larry M. Eig, at 14-15. Within the CFP Act there are numerous examples of the term "title" being used in what appear to be appropriate times, along with apparently apt uses of the term "subtitle." One notable example is in the way that the CFP Act delineates: (1) the CFPB's authority to prescribe rules declaring acts or practices pertaining to covered consumer financial products or services to be unlawful because they are unfair, deceptive, or abusive (Dodd-Frank Act §§1031, 1036, 12 U.S.C. §§5531, 5536); and (2) the FTC's mandate to prohibit unfair and deceptive "acts or practices in or affecting commerce." (15 U.S.C. §45). Because these powers are so similar, the CFP Act carefully defines the limits of the FTC's and CFPB's jurisdictions and how they are to interact in instances where their authorities overlap. To accomplish this, there are numerous references to "title" and "subtitle" that strongly indicate that each word was chosen with care. See Dodd-Frank Act §1061(b)(5), 12 U.S.C. §5581(b)(5).

[124] See, e.g., Dodd-Frank Act §1002(14), 12 U.S.C. §5481(14) ("The term 'Federal Consumer Financial Law' means the provisions of this title, the enumerated consumer laws, the laws for which authorities are transferred under subtitles F and H, and any rule or order prescribed by the Bureau under this title, an enumerated consumer law, or pursuant to the authorities transferred under subtitles F and H. The term does not include the Federal Trade Commission Act."). See also CRS Report 97-589, *Statutory Interpretation: General Principles and Recent Trends*, by Larry M. Eig, at 14- 15.

[125] For example, subtitle F provides that the FRB's rulemaking authorities under the TILA shall be transferred to the Bureau. Section 1100A of subtitle H amends TILA to effectuate the transfer of authorities by, for example, replacing all relevant references to the FRB with references to the "Bureau."

[126] Dodd-Frank Act §§1027(b), (c), (d), (e), (f), (g), (h), and (*l*), 12 U.S.C. §§5517(b), (c), (d), (e), (f), (g), (h), and (*l*) (emphasis added). In addition to the plain meaning of the statutory text, the location of the Secretary's authorizing provision seems to indicate a legislative intent to constrict his power to exercise the Bureau's transferred authorities. It seems that subtitle A, which establishes the Bureau and the office of the Director and provides the Director with executive and administrative authorities, would be a more logical location for an authorization to the Secretary to perform all of the Director's powers until a valid appointment.

[127] H.R. 3126, 111th Cong. §§112 and 166. See also Mike Ferullo, *Frank Offers Revised Legislation to Create Consumer Agency; Hearing Set for Sept. 30*, Bureau of Nat'l Affairs, Inc., Oct. 1, 2009.

[128] See *Mark-Up of Discussion Draft of the consumer Financial Protection Agency Act of 2009 (to be reported as H.R. 3126) Before the H. Comm. on Fin. Serv.*, 111th Cong. (2009), materials available at http://archives.financialservices.house.gov/ Hearings/hearing Details.aspx?NewsID=801.

[129] H.REPT. 111-367. See also *Markup of H.R. 3126, the Consumer Financial Protection Agency Act of 2009 Before the H. Comm,. on Energy and Commerce*, 111th Cong. (2009), materials available at http://energycommerce.house.gov/ news/PRArticle.aspx?NewsID=7531.

[130] This provision would have raised constitutional concerns had it been enacted.

[131] H.R. 4173, 111th Cong. § 4102 (as passed by House, Dec. 11, 2009) (emphasis added). After an initial period in which the proposed consumer agency would have been run either by a

single acting director or a single appointed director, the leadership structure of the agency would convert to a five-member commission. *Id.*

[132] The Dodd-Frank Act's conference report does not synthesize the legislative language. H.R. REP. 111-517. The report ordered by the Banking Committee stated: "Section 1066 provides the Secretary of the Treasury authority to perform the functions of the Bureau under the CFP Act until the Director of the Bureau is confirmed by the Senate." S.Rept. 111-176, at 178.

[133] TILA, for instance, was originally enacted in 1968, while RESPA originally was signed into law in 1974.

[134] The Secretary, in consultation with other regulators, was required to establish the designated transfer date between 180 days and 18 months after the date of enactment, July 21, 2010. Dodd-Frank Act §1062, 12 U.S.C. §5582.

[135] Legal challenges might be initiated by a covered financial institution seeking to prevent the Bureau from exercising an authority specifically against it, or by the Bureau seeking a court order compelling an institution to comply with a law or regulation. As previously discussed, it would appear the de facto officer doctrine is not likely to be applied to timely, direct challenges of actions performed under the direction of Cordray because they would raise significant constitutional issues.

[136] The authorities also may be exercised by a duly authorized delegatee of the Secretary's. The Secretary has broad discretionary authority to "delegate duties and powers of the Secretary to another officer or employee of the Department of the Treasury." 31 U.S.C. §321(b). Under this provision, the Secretary presumably could hire Richard Cordray as an officer of the Treasury Department and delegate to Cordray his CFPB powers.

[137] The Secretary would not be bound by the actions taken under Cordray's leadership. Consequently, the Secretary could ratify each of these rules exactly how they previously were issued under Cordray, issue similar rules with changes, or altogether rescind certain rules.

[138] The Bureau provides links to all final and proposed rules at http://www.consumerfinance.gov/regulations/. Notable rulemakings issued under Cordray's leadership include Loan Originator Compensation Requirements under the Truth in Lending Act (Regulation Z), 78 Fed. Reg. 11,279 (Feb. 15, 2013) (to be codified at 12 C.F.R. Part 1026); Mortgage Servicing Rules under the Real Estate Settlement Procedures Act (Regulation X), 78 Fed. Reg. 10,696 (Feb. 14, 2013) (to be codified at 12 C.F.R. Part 1024); Mortgage Servicing Rules under the Truth in Lending Act (Regulation Z), 78 Fed. Reg. 10,092 (Feb. 14, 2013) (to be codified at 12 C.F.R. Part 1026); and Ability-to-Repay and Qualified Mortgage Standards under the Truth in Lending Act (Regulation Z), 78 Fed. Reg. 6,408 (Jan. 30, 2013) (to be codified at 12 C.F.R. Part 1026).

[139] Electronic Fund Transfers, 77 Fed. Reg. 6194 (Feb. 7, 2012) (to be codified at 12 C.F.R. Part 1005). The Bureau has made several amendments to the February final rule. See *Remittance Transfer Rule (Amendment to Regulation E)*, available at http://www.consumerfinance.gov/regulations/final-remittance-rule-amendment-regulation-e/.

[140] 15 U.S.C. §§1601, *et seq.*

[141] 12 U.S.C. §§2601, *et seq.*

[142] These Dodd-Frank Act provisions were drafted as amendments to the three enumerated consumer laws (TILA, RESPA, and EFTA). Dodd-Frank Act section 1400 expressly provides that the relevant mortgage-related provisions of Title XIV "shall be enumerated consumer laws, as defined in section 1002 [of the CFP Act], and shall come under the purview of the Bureau of Consumer Financial Protection for purposes of title X, including the transfer of functions and personnel under subtitle F of title X and the savings provisions of such subtitle." Dodd-Frank Act §1400, 12 U.S.C. §1601(note). Additionally, the authority to implement these amendments was provided to the relevant transferor agencies until the designated transfer date.

[143] Defining Larger Participants of the Consumer Reporting Market, 77 Fed. Reg. 42,874 (July 20, 2012) (to be codified at 12 C.F.R. Part 1090).

[144] Defining Larger Participants of the Consumer Debt Collection Market, 77 Fed. Reg. 65,775 (Oct. 31, 2012) (to be codified at 12 C.F.R. Part 1090).

[145] Dodd-Frank Act §1024(a)(1)(B), 12 U.S.C. §5514(a)(1)(B).

[146] The CFPB also has issued final interpretative rules and rules involving internal Bureau procedures and policies. It seems unlikely that these rules could cause a personalized injury sufficient for a plaintiff to have legal standing to challenge their validity.

[147] *Stipulation and Consent Order*, In the Matter of: Capital One Bank, (USA) N.A., Consumer Fin. Prot. Bureau, July 18, 2012; *Joint Consent Order, Joint Order for Restitution, and Joint Order to Pay Civil Money Penalty*, In the Matter of: American Express Centurion Bank, Fed. Deposit Ins. Co. and Consumer Fin. Prot. Bureau, Oct. 1, 2012; *Consent Order, Order for Restitution, and Order to Pay Civil Money Penalty*, In the Matter of: American Express Bank, FSB, Consumer Fin. Prot. Bureau, Oct. 1, 2012; *Consent Order, Order for Restitution, and Order to Pay Civil Money Penalty*, In the Matter of: American Express Travel Related Services Company, Inc., Consumer Fin. Prot. Bureau, Oct. 1, 2012; and *Joint Consent Order, Order for Restitution, and Order to Pay Civil Money Penalty*, In the Matter of Discover Bank, Fed. Deposit Ins. Co. and Consumer Fin. Prot. Bureau, Sept. 24, 2012. These orders and other administrative adjudication materials pertaining to the Bureau are available at http://www.consumerfinance.gov/ administrativeadjudication/.

[148] The orders were against either a larger depository directly or a third-party service provider of a larger depository, which is subject to the Bureau's regulatory authority to the same extent as a larger depository. Dodd-Frank Act §1025(d), 12 U.S.C. §5515(d).

[149] Dodd-Frank Act §§1031, 1036, 12 U.S.C. §§5531, 5536.

In: Recess Appointment Power
Editor: Chase N. Morrison
ISBN: 978-1-62948-675-8

Chapter 3

RECESS APPOINTMENTS: A LEGAL OVERVIEW*

Vivian S. Chu

SUMMARY

The U.S. Constitution explicitly provides the President with two methods of appointing officers of the United States. First, the Appointments Clause provides the President with the authority to make appointments with the advice and consent of the Senate. Specifically, Article II, Section 2, clause 2 states that the President "shall nominate, and by and with the Advice and Consent of the Senate, shall appoint Ambassadors, other public Ministers and Consuls, Judges of the supreme Court, and all other Officers of the United States, whose Appointments are not herein otherwise provided for, and which shall be established by law." Second, the Recess Appointments Clause authorizes the President to make temporary appointments unilaterally during periods when the Senate is not in session. Article II, Section 2, clause 3 provides: "The President shall have Power to fill up all Vacancies that may happen during the Recess of the Senate, by granting Commissions which shall expire at the End of their next Session."

While the Recess Appointments Clause enables the continuity of government operations, Presidents, on occasion, have exercised authority

* This is an edited, reformatted and augmented version of a Congressional Research Service publication, CRS Report for Congress RL33009, dated July 19, 2013.

under the Clause for tactical or political purposes, appointing officials who might otherwise have difficulty securing Senate confirmation. The Recess Appointments Clause is not without its ambiguities, and the President's use of this power in light of these ambiguities has given rise to significant political and legal controversy since the beginning of the republic.

This report provides an overview of the Recess Appointments Clause, exploring its historical application and legal interpretation by the executive branch, the courts, and the Comptroller General. It also reflects the U.S. Court of Appeals for the D.C. Circuit's decision in *Noel Canning v. Nat'l Labor Relations Board*, which held that the President's three recess appointments to the National Labor Relations Board (NLRB) on January 4, 2012, were invalid. Furthermore, congressional legislation designed to prevent the President's overuse or misuse of the Clause is also explored.

CONSTITUTIONAL ORIGINS

The Appointments Clause of the Constitution establishes that the President "shall nominate, and by and with the Advice and Consent of the Senate, shall appoint Ambassadors, other public Ministers and Consuls, Judges of the supreme Court, and all other Officers of the United States, whose Appointments are not herein otherwise provided for and which shall be established by law."[1] Pursuant to the Recess Appointments Clause, the President, further, has the "Power to fill up all Vacancies that may happen during the Recess of the Senate, by granting Commissions which shall expire at the End of their next Session."[2] The Recess Appointments Clause was adopted by the Constitutional Convention without dissent or debate regarding the intent and scope of its terms.

In light of express provisions and historical pronouncements during ratification of the Constitution, it has been generally accepted that the Recess Appointments Clause was designed to enable the President to ensure the unfettered operation of the government during periods when the Senate was not in session and therefore unable to perform its advice and consent function.[3] Alexander Hamilton referred to the recess appointment power as "nothing more than a supplement ... for the purpose of establishing an auxiliary method of appointment, in cases to which the general method was inadequate."[4] During the ratification debates in Pennsylvania, Thomas McKean, a prominent figure of the American Revolution and member of the Pennsylvania convention, noted with approval the sharing of the appointive power with the

Senate and stated that the Senate need not "be under any necessity of sitting constantly, as has been alleged, for there is an express provision made to enable the President to fill up all vacancies that may happen during their recess; the commissions, to expire at the end of the next session."[5] Likewise, Archibald Maclaine, a member of the Hillsborough convention during the ratification debates in North Carolina and influential supporter for ratification of the Constitution, stated:

> Congress are not to be sitting at all times; they will only sit from time to time, as the public business may render it necessary. Therefore the executive ought to make temporary appointments.... This power can be vested nowhere but in the executive, because he is perpetually acting for the public; for, though the Senate is to advise him in the appointment of officers, &c., yet, during the recess, the President must do this business, or else it will be neglected; and such neglect may occasion public inconveniences.[6]

These declarations, however, do not definitively indicate how the recess appointment power should be interpreted. For example, should it be interpreted narrowly, such that only very limited circumstances trigger its use, or broadly, such that various circumstances trigger its use? With the inherent ambiguities of the Clause, and the evolution of modern congressional practices,[7] the confusion over recess appointments is further complicated by additional factors, such as the application of statutory restrictions to recess appointments. Accordingly, this report first reviews early congressional scheduling and presidential recess appointments and then examines the textual and historical interpretation of the ambiguous phrases of the Recess Appointments Clause—that is, "Vacancies that may happen" and "the Recess of the Senate."

This report also addresses the U.S. Court of Appeals for the D.C. Circuit's (D.C. Circuit's) analysis of the Recess Appointments Clause in *Noel Canning v. Nat'l Labor Relations Board*,[8] which held that President Obama's recess appointments to the National Labor Relations Board (NLRB) on January 4, 2012, were unconstitutional. Notably, the Supreme Court has granted *certiorari* to review the *Noel Canning* decision in the forthcoming 2013 term.[9] The circumstances of President Obama's January 4, 2012, recess appointments to the NLRB and the Consumer Financial Protection Bureau (CFPB) are discussed in further detail below (*see infra* "Congressional Scheduling Practice"). Notably, however, the unique facts underlying these appointments have rekindled debate regarding the meaning of key phrases in the Recess

Appointments Clause, as discussed below, and have raised new questions, such as which branch—the executive or legislative—has the ability to determine when the Senate is in recess. The potential impact on the relationship between the President and Congress in the wake of the *Noel Canning* decision is beyond the scope of this report.[10] The authority and tenure of recess appointees are then discussed, followed by a review of congressional action to curb potentially politically motivated utilization of the recess appointment power.

CONGRESSIONAL SCHEDULING AND EARLY PRESIDENTIAL USE

The ambiguities of the Clause and how it should be interpreted are complicated by the fact that the congressional schedule and travel limitations it appears to have been designed to address have undergone tremendous change since the founding period. Until the Civil War, Congress consistently met for relatively short sessions followed by long recesses, or breaks, of six to nine months; this historical practice appears to support the idea of the recess appointment power as a practical accommodation.[11] Congress largely adhered to this practice during and after the Civil War, scheduling an "intrasession recess"[12] of approximately two weeks from the end of December until the beginning of January.[13] The recess practices of Congress changed in the mid-20th century, and are now characterized by more frequent recesses of relatively short duration within a session of Congress. The length of "intersession recesses," that is, the adjournment between sessions of Congress, has also become shorter.[14]

Interpretations of the Clause have also been complicated by the evolution of its use by successive Presidents. In addition to fostering administrative continuity, Presidents have exercised authority under the Recess Appointments Clause for tactical or political purposes throughout the history of the republic, giving rise to significant political and legal controversy. For instance, President Madison's recess appointments of Albert Gallatin, John Quincy Adams, and James A. Bayard as envoys to negotiate a peace treaty with Great Britain in 1813 prompted heated debate in the Senate.[15] Presidents Jackson, Taylor, and Lincoln also made hundreds of recess appointments during their terms.[16] Additionally, recess appointments to the judiciary were common during the early years of the republic, with the first five Presidents making 31 such appointments, including 5 to the Supreme Court.[17] Among these, President Washington's recess appointment of John Rutledge as Chief Justice generated significant controversy, ultimately factoring in his rejection by the Senate.[18] Interestingly, there is no recorded challenge to the constitutionality of his recess appointment.[19] In total, 12 Justices have received recess appointments to the Supreme Court, and many of these Justices participated in Court business prior to Senate action on their nominations.[20]

The mid-19th century phenomena of long congressional adjournments, frequent resort to recess appointments, and the rise of the spoils system[21] in the federal government spurred Congress to impose statutory restrictions on the President's appointment and removal power, including restrictions on paying certain classes of recess appointees.[22] Additionally, the Tenure of Office Act of 1867, which figured prominently in the impeachment effort against President Andrew Johnson, included several provisions purporting to limit the recess appointment power of the President.[23]

TEXTUAL ISSUES AND HISTORICAL INTERPRETATION

Although practices with respect to recess appointments and debates between Presidents and Congress over the propriety of particular recess appointments occurred in the formative years of the republic,[24] formal consideration of the issue has occurred primarily in the context of Attorneys General opinions, with periodic attention from the courts and Congress. Aspects of the recess appointment power were considered as early as 1792, and there were at least 19 formal Attorneys General opinions in the 19th century on recess appointments, the earliest being in 1823. Interpretation questions have primarily revolved around the phrases "Vacancies that may happen" and "the Recess of the Senate," as the meaning of these phrases indicates when the Clause may be used by the President to make these temporary appointments. Accordingly, these phrases are discussed in this section.

Although some of the interpretational questions surrounding the Recess Appointments Clause have been deemed to be settled by the executive branch, there have been numerous contrary opinions and expressions of doubt in the course of arriving at the interpretation that has prevailed for over 100 years. More recently, a decision from the U.S. Court of Appeals for the D.C. Circuit (D.C. Circuit) issued on January 25, 2013, appears to resurrect a formalist interpretation of the Clause that has long been rejected by various federal courts of appeals and the executive branch.[25]

RECESS APPOINTMENTS CLAUSE (ART. II, §2, CL. 3.)

The President shall have Power to fill up all *Vacancies that may happen* during the *Recess of the Senate*, by granting Commissions which shall expire at the End of their next Session (emphasis added).

"Vacancies That May Happen"

An initial question that arose was what constitutes a "Vacanc[y] that may happen" during the recess of the Senate—that is, must a vacancy to which the Recess Appointments Clause applies come into existence during the recess, or may it be a vacancy that is already in existence when the recess occurs? The interpretations of the executive branch are first discussed, followed by judicial opinions that have examined this phrase.

Attorneys General Interpretations

On the one hand, if the term "happen" is interpreted as referring only to vacancies that come into being during a recess, or arise after a recess of the Senate commences, it necessarily follows that the President would lack authority to make a recess appointment to a vacancy that existed prior to the recess. In 1792, the first Attorney General, Edmund J. Randolph, responded to an inquiry as to whether a recess appointment could be made to the position of Chief Coiner of the Mint, a newly created position for which no nomination had been made before the Senate recessed.[26] Attorney General Randolph concluded that the vacancy occurred on the day the office had been created, and thus could not be filled with a recess appointment because the vacancy existed prior to the Senate's recess.[27] He based his opinion on the text of the Clause and on the "spirit of the Constitution," declaring that the Recess Appointments Clause must be "interpreted strictly" because it serves as "an exception to the general participation of the Senate."[28] In 1799, Alexander Hamilton, then serving as Major General of the Army, responded to a similar inquiry from the Secretary of War, stating "[i]t is clear, that independent of the authority of a special law, the President cannot fill a vacancy [pursuant to the

Recess Appointments Clause] which happens during a session of the Senate."[29]

On the other hand, if "happen" is construed more broadly to encompass all vacancies that exist during a recess, then the President would be empowered to make a recess appointment to any vacant position, irrespective of when the position becomes vacant. In 1823, Attorney General William Wirt, without mentioning the Randolph opinion, concluded that the phrase encompassed all vacancies that happen to exist during "the Recess."[30] Under this interpretation, recess appointments could be made to vacancies that come into being before the recess of the Senate commences. Although Attorney General Wirt acknowledged that the "opposite construction [i.e., Randolph's narrower interpretation] is, perhaps, more strictly consonant with the mere letter" of the Clause, he opted for, in his view, "the only construction of the Constitution which is compatible with its spirit, reason, and purpose."[31] Attorney General Wirt further stated, "The substantial purpose of the Constitution was to keep these offices filled; and powers adequate to this purpose were intended to be conveyed. But if the President shall not have the power to fill a vacancy thus circumstanced, the powers are inadequate to the purpose, and the substance of the Constitution will be sacrificed to a dubious construction of its letter."[32]

During thc 19th century, Members of the Senate also held conflicting views regarding the interpretation of "Vacancies that may happen."[33] Other notable scholars such as Joseph Story, in his *Commentaries on the Constitution*, seemed to adopt a construction different from Wirt's, at least with respect to newly created offices to which nominations had not been named (akin to the Randolph position).[34] Differing interpretations, such as those of Attorneys General Randolph and Wirt, are reflective of the early controversies between the Senate and the President on the meaning of this phrase.

Subsequent opinions of the Attorneys General in 1832 and 1841 endorsed Wirt's interpretation.[35] Echoing the sentiments of Wirt, Attorney General Roger B. Taney, in the 1832 opinion, stated that the Constitution "was formed for practical purposes, and a construction that defeats the very object of the grant of power cannot be the true one. It was the intention of the constitution that the offices created by law, and necessary to carry on the operations of the government, should always be full, or at all events, that the vacancy should not be a protracted one."[36] He went on to stress, however, that "vacancies are not *designedly* to be kept open by the President until the recess, for the purpose of avoiding the control of the Senate."[37]

Notwithstanding the opinions that agreed with the 1832 Wirt opinion, the interpretation of "Vacancies that may happen" by the Attorneys General returned to the narrower construction for a short time. In a brief opinion from 1845, Attorney General John Y. Mason concluded that "[i]f vacancies are known to exist during the session of the Senate, and nominations are not then made, they cannot be filled by executive appointments in the recess of the Senate."[38] He also stated that "[f]rom the commencement of the government, it is believed that a power has been exercised which would appear to be inconsistent with a construction of the section of the constitution which would confine the meaning of the word 'happen' to the time at which the office is in fact vacated."[39] Also, during this period, several Senators raised questions as to the proper interpretation of the word "happen" in the Recess Appointments Clause. A Senate Committee on the Judiciary Report from 1863 expressed that vacancies that arose while the Senate was in session could not be filled by recess appointment;[40] however, other Members noted that contrary opinions existed on the subject.

Despite this brief departure from the broader interpretation of Attorney General Wirt, formal Attorneys General opinions returned to the Wirt interpretation beginning in 1855. These opinions further concluded that "Vacancies may happen" included newly created offices that had never been filled.[41] Attorney General Edward Bates, in an 1862 opinion, stated that the question of when a vacancy may happen "is settled ... as far, at least, as a constitutional question can be settled, by the continued practice of your predecessors, and the reiterated opinions of mine, and sanctioned, as far as I know or believe, by the unbroken acquiescence of the Senate."[42] Attorney General Henry Stanberry also justified his interpretation by noting that the term vacancy "implies duration, a condition or state of things which may exist for a period of time. Can it be said that the word *happen*, when applied to such a subject, is only properly applicable to its beginning?"[43] Stanberry further stated that executive power must always have capacity for action and that to adopt a narrow construction of the Recess Appointments Clause would interfere with that ability.[44] Attorney General Evarts, in an 1868 opinion, declared the matter so settled by his predecessors that it was "hardly useful to express an opinion as upon an original question."[45] Subsequent Attorneys General opinions have consistently interpreted "happen" to mean "happen to exist" and have acknowledged recess appointments to offices that became vacant while the Senate was in session.[46]

Furthermore, an appropriations rider to prevent recess appointees from being paid was enacted. This early pay restriction prevented payment of a salary to any recess appointee filling a vacancy that "existed while the Senate was in session and is by law required to be filled by the advice and consent of the Senate."[47] However, exceptions were later enacted that permitted recess appointees to be paid under certain circumstances.[48] (*See infra* "Modern Statutory Pay Restriction (5 U.S.C. §5503)"). The early version of the pay restriction could indicate congressional objection to the interpretation that a vacancy, for purposes of the Recess Appointments Clause, is any vacancy that exists when the Senate is in "the Recess." Alternatively, the enactment of the exceptions could indicate congressional understanding or acceptance of this long-standing interpretation.

Judicial Interpretations

Courts have occasionally examined the Recess Appointments Clause, but the broader interpretation of "Vacanc[y] that may happen" was first adopted by a federal court in the 1880 decision *In re Farrow*.[49] In *Farrow*, Circuit Justice Woods adopted the reasoning of the aforementioned Attorneys General opinions, stating that "[t]hese opinions exhaust all that can be said on the subject."[50] In reaching his conclusion, Circuit Justice Woods rejected the contrary opinion of a district court, stating that its holding "ought not to be held to outweigh the authority of the great number which are cited in support of the opposite view, and of the practice of the executive department for nearly 60 years, the acquiescence of the [S]enate therein, and the recognition of the power claimed by both [H]ouses of [C]ongress."[51] The holding in *Farrow* was also subsequently echoed in the 1886 decision *In re Yancey*.[52]

In the modern era, courts have continued to adhere to this interpretation. In *United States v. Allocco*, for instance, the U.S. Court of Appeals for the Second Circuit (Second Circuit) stated that a contrary interpretation "would create executive paralysis and do violence to the orderly functioning of our complex government."[53] Likewise, in *United States v. Woodley*, the U.S. Court of Appeals for the Ninth Circuit (Ninth Circuit) stated that a narrow interpretation would "lead to the absurd result that all offices vacant on the day the Senate recesses would have to remain vacant at least until the Senate reconvenes."[54] In *Evans v. Stephens*, the U.S. Court of Appeals for the Eleventh Circuit (Eleventh Circuit) stated that "interpreting the phrase to prohibit the President from filling a vacancy that comes into being on the last day of a Session but to empower the President to fill a vacancy that arises immediately thereafter (on the first day of a recess) contradicts what we understand to be the purpose of the Recess Appointments Clause: to keep important offices filled and the government functioning."[55] In addition to highlighting the practical problems that could result should a narrow interpretation be favored, these decisions principally focused on evaluating historical precedent and practice, including the "long and continuous line of [Attorneys General] opinions" and the "widespread acceptance of the practice followed since the earliest days of the Republic."[56]

In contrast to these holdings from the Second, Ninth, and Eleventh Circuits, the D.C. Circuit in *Noel Canning v. Nat'l Labor Relations Board* favored the narrower construction. It held "that the President may only make recess appointments to fill vacancies that arise during the recess."[57] The court further concluded that the "vacancy" for purposes of the Clause must be one that arises after the Senate enters "the Recess," which, in the court's view, occurs when the Senate adjourns *sine die*.[58] (*See infra* "The Recess of the Senate" and "Authority and Tenure of Recess Appointees.")

The D.C. Circuit arrived at a narrower construction because, in a textual analysis of the phrase, it reasoned that the term "happen" cannot encompass all vacancies in existence; otherwise "the operative phrase 'that may happen' would be wholly unnecessary."[59] It criticized its sister circuits for relying on modern dictionaries to define "happen," rather than contemporary 18th century dictionaries that defined the term as understood during the time of ratification.[60] It also turned to the Senate Vacancies Clause, which at the time of ratification, stated, "if Vacancies happen by Resignation, or otherwise, during the Recess of the Legislature of any State, the Executive thereof may make temporary appointments ..."[61] Finding this phraseology similar to the Recess Appointments Clause, the court found the Senate Vacancies Clause "makes sense if 'happen ... during the Recess' refers to arising or coming into being during 'the Recess.' If it merely means that the vacancy happens to exist at the time of a recess, it becomes implausible."[62] Furthermore, the court interpreted early historical commentary by Attorney General Randolph and Alexander Hamilton, discussed above, as supporting the principle that the recess appointment power provided to the President is primarily a "secondary method" that, if read broadly, would eviscerate "the primary mode of appointments set forth in [the Appointments Clause]."[63]

While the *Allocco*, *Woodley*, and *Evans* decisions each emphasized the functional purpose of their interpretations, the *Noel Canning* court suggested that any arguably "dire consequences" that could arise as a result of its narrower interpretation could be remedied by Congress amending statutes to provide for extended service of an officeholder until the qualification of a successor.[64] The D.C. Circuit also rejected the argument that Congress acquiesced in the practice of making recess appointments to existing vacancies based on the statute that restricts a recess appointee's salary, finding that one branch's assent to a practice does not preclude it from judicial review.[65]

Summary

With respect to this particular phrase, Attorneys General and several courts have rejected a narrow interpretation and have adopted the broader construction, believing it to be both consistent with the spirit of the Clause and necessary for the continuous and efficient operation of the government. It has also been argued that the Congress has acquiesced in this interpretation, primarily through the passage of statutes that recognize the possibility of such appointments, discussed below.[66] While a broader interpretation of this phrase has been supported for over 100 years, congressional statements disputing the prevailing interpretation have been made during periods of controversy surrounding recess appointments. Notably, such statements have been made by "individual members of the senate ... but not the senate itself."[67] Moreover, the D.C. Circuit's decision in *Noel Canning*, applying "Vacancies that may happen" only to vacancies that arise during "the Recess," may rekindle debate on the circumstances under which the President may exercise his recess appointment power.

"The Recess of the Senate"

As discussed above, the traditionally prevailing interpretation—notwithstanding the *Noel Canning* decision—has been that the President may exercise his recess appointment power regardless of whether a vacancy occurs before or during the recess of the Senate. The question of what constituted a recess for purposes of the Clause arose substantially later than the vacancy issue due to the fact that adjournments within Senate sessions were infrequent and of short duration in the early days of the republic.[68] As congressional scheduling evolved and such intrasession recesses became longer and more frequent, the opportunity for such appointments increased. Accordingly, the interpretation of this phrase for purposes of the Clause—that is, to what period of time does "the Recess" refer—has become more critical.

Attorneys General Interpretation

The first formal opinion on the subject was issued by Attorney General Philander C. Knox in 1901, and he concluded that the phrase applied only to adjournments between sessions of Congress, commonly referred to as "intersession" recesses.[69] Attorney General Knox placed significant weight on the use of the definite article "the" in the Recess Appointments Clause, emphasizing that "[i]t will be observed that the phrase is '*the* recess.'"[70] The opinion further concluded that if recess appointments were allowed during periods other than an intersession recess, nothing would prevent an appointment from being made "during any adjournment, as from Thursday or Friday until the following Monday."[71] The opinion specifically rejected a U.S. Court of Claims decision that upheld paying the salary of an Army paymaster appointed during a temporary (intrasession) recess in 1867, which had extended from July 20 to November 21, 1867.[72]

This position was abandoned 20 years later. An opinion issued by Attorney General Harry M. Daugherty in 1921 declared that an appointment made during a 29-day intrasession recess was constitutional.[73] Similar to the opinions supporting a broad interpretation of "Vacancies that may happen," the Daugherty opinion focused on the practical aspects of the recess appointment dynamic. It stated that "[i]f the President's power of appointment is to be defeated because the Senate takes an adjournment to a specified date, the painful and inevitable result will be measurably to prevent the exercise of governmental functions."[74] In support of this interpretation, Attorney General Daugherty cited the 1884 Court of Claims decision that had been repudiated in the Knox opinion, as well as a report from 1905 of the Senate Committee on the Judiciary that specifically examined the meaning of the term "recess." Although the Senate report did not specifically address intrasession recess appointments, it had concluded:

> It was evidently intended by the framers of the Constitution that it [Article II, sec. 2] should mean something real, not something imaginary; something actual, not something fictitious. They used the word as the mass of mankind then understood it and now understand it. It means, in our judgment, in this connection the period of time when the Senate is *not sitting in regular or extraordinary session as a branch of the Congress or in extraordinary session for the discharge of executive functions;* when its members owe no duty of attendance; when its chamber is empty; when, because of its absence, it can not receive communications from the President or participate as a body in making appointments.... This is essentially a proviso to the provision relative to appointments by and with the advice and consent of the Senate. It was carefully devised so as to accomplish the purpose in view, without in the slightest degree changing the policy of the Constitution, that such appointments are only to be made with the participation of the Senate. Its sole purpose was to render it certain that at all times there should be, whether the Senate was in session

or not, an officer for every office, entitled to discharge the duties thereof.[75]

Even though he emphasized this functional approach, Attorney General Daugherty limited the scope of his opinion by rejecting the notion that a broad interpretation would authorize intrasession appointments during brief adjournments, declaring that "an adjournment for 5 or even 10 days [cannot] be said to constitute the recess intended by the Constitution."[76] The opinion concluded by emphasizing that while "[e]very presumption is to be indulged in favor of the validity of whatever action [the President] may take ..., there is a point, necessarily hard of definition, where palpable abuse of discretion might subject his appointment to review."[77]

Notably, the 1905 Senate Committee on the Judiciary Report, quoted above and relied on by Attorney General Daugherty in his 1921 opinion, was prompted by what undoubtedly was the briefest recess ever relied on by a President in order to make recess appointments. In the 58th Congress, the first session ended at noon—December 7, 1903—and the second session immediately began thereafter.[78] During the moment between the two sessions, President Theodore Roosevelt announced the recess appointment of over 160 officers—mostly military.[79] The period between these sessions was construed by Roosevelt's Administration as a "constructive recess."[80] The 1905 Senate Committee on the Judiciary Report was issued 14 months afterward and emphatically rejected Roosevelt's actions. It is possible that the report, while expressing disapprobation of the President's exercise of the recess appointment power in such a manner, could be read as validating the execution of intrasession recess appointments generally. Alternatively, it could be argued that this historically anomalous event lends no weight to the overall consideration of the matter.[81] Subsequent Attorneys General and Department of Justice Office of Legal Counsel opinions have continued to support the constitutionality of intrasession recess appointments.[82] Other Department of Justice pronouncements on the issue also strongly imply that the Clause encompasses all recesses in excess of three days.[83]

To a minor degree, the pocket veto case, *Kennedy v. Samspon*, has arguably influenced the propriety of recess appointments during short intrasession recesses of the Senate.[84] The Constitution provides that a bill becomes law if not returned by the President after presentment within 10 days, "unless the Congress by their adjournment prevent its return, in which case it shall not be a law."[85] In *Kennedy*, the court struck down the exercise of the President's pocket veto power during a six-day adjournment, or intrasession recess, of the Congress. *Kennedy* cast doubt on the validity of all intrasession pocket vetoes, not only those of short duration; Presidents have since limited their pocket vetoes to the periods between sessions, or after a Congress has finally adjourned.[86] In light of the *Kennedy* decision, the Department of Justice, while asserting the validity of a recess appointment during a 33-day intrasession recess, nevertheless informed President Carter that "in view of the functional affinity between the pocket veto and recess appointment powers, Presidents during recent years have been hesitant to make recess appointments during intrasession recesses of the Senate."[87]

Although the decision in *Kennedy* may have moderated the use of the recess appointment power in some instances, recent Presidents have nonetheless made numerous appointments during intrasession recesses of 10 days or longer.[88]

- President Reagan, for instance, made a number of intrasession recess appointments, one during a 19-day recess ending September 8, 1982, nine during a 24-day recess ending on July 23, 1984, and two during a 14-day recess ending on January 21, 1985.
- President George H. W. Bush made eight intrasession recess appointments, the shortest occurring during an 18-day recess.
- President Clinton made numerous intrasession appointments, including five during a 12-day recess ending on January 22, 1996, five during a 17-day recess ending on April 15, 1996, one during a 10-day recess ending on June 3, 1996, and one during a 12-day recess ending on January 20, 2001.
- President George W. Bush continued the practice of making appointments during brief intrasession recesses, including six such appointments during an 18-day recess ending on April 28, 2003, four during a 11-day recess ending on April 19, 2004, and, perhaps most controversially, the appointment of William H. Pryor Jr. to the Court of Appeals for the Eleventh Circuit on February 20, 2004, on the seventh day of an 11-day recess ending on February 23, 2004.[89]
- President Barack Obama has also made some intrasession recess appointments. As of March 8, 2013, President Obama had made 32 recess appointments, 22 of which were made during intrasession recesses during the second session of the 111th Congress. Many intrasession recess appointments were made during arguably lengthy recesses of the Senate; however, President Obama made three recess

appointments on July 7, 2010, during a 12-day recess ending July 12, 2010.[90]

Judicial Interpretation

In 2004, the Eleventh Circuit upheld President George W. Bush's recess appointment of William H. Pryor Jr. to the federal court of appeals during a 10-day intrasession recess. As it did with interpreting "Vacanc[y] that may happen," the Eleventh Circuit focused on historical practice and discussed the main purpose of the Clause, which is "to enable the President to fill vacancies to assure the proper functioning of our government."[91] It also rejected the argument that the definite article—"the"—limited the opportunity to make an appointment to one particular recess.[92] The Eleventh Circuit was the first appellate court to hold that "the Recess," for purposes of the Recess Appointments Clause, includes an intrasession recess. Under this interpretation, the court also addressed arguments that an intrasession recess must be a minimum number of days. On this issue, it stated:

> The Constitution, on its face, does not establish a minimum time that an authorized break in the Senate must last to give legal force to the President's appointment power under the Recess Appointments Clause. And we do not set that limit today. Although a President has not before appointed a judge to an Article III court during an intrasession recess as short as the one in this case, appointments to other offices—offices ordinarily requiring Senate confirmation—have been made during an intrasession recess of about this length or shorter. Furthermore, several times in the past, fairly short intrasession recesses have given rise to presidential appointments of judges to Article III courts.[93]

Although interpretation of "the Recess of the Senate" appeared largely to have been consistent across the federal circuits, the D.C. Circuit in *Noel Canning* held that "the Recess" is limited to intersession recesses.[94] Based on a textual analysis, the D.C. Circuit found the definite article—"the"—significant because its use indicates a particular recess, not any adjournment or "generic break in proceedings."[95]According to the court, "[t]he natural interpretation of the Clause is that the Constitution is noting a difference between 'the Recess' and the 'Session.' Either the Senate is in session or it is in the recess."[96] Like the Eleventh Circuit, the D.C. Circuit looked at historical practice, however, it concentrated on the absence of intrasession recess appointments within the first 80 years after the Constitution's ratification, which suggested "an assumed absence of [the] power" to make such appointments.[97] The court found its interpretation strengthened by a lack of viable alternative interpretations. Most notably, the D.C. Circuit rejected Attorney General Daugherty's functionalist interpretation from 1921, "in favor of the clarity of the intersession interpretation" and because the text of the Clause offers "no support for the functional approach."[98] In addition, the court also rejected the interpretation that "the Recess" means "any adjournment of more than three days pursuant to the Adjournments Clause."[99] Emphasizing that the word "adjournment" is not used in the Recess Appointments Clause, and finding no historical evidence to suggest a link between the two Clauses, the D.C. Circuit concluded it could not "read one as governing the other," and would not "ignor[e] the Framers' choice of words."[100]

Moreover, the D.C. Circuit concluded that the Senate only enters "the Recess," or intersession recess, for purposes of the Clause when it adjourns *sine die*.[101] This conclusion, in conjunction with the court's interpretation of "Vacanc[y] that may happen," would mean that a President would be limited in making appointments to those vacancies that arise during an intersession recess in which the Senate adjourns *sine die*, and the vacancies may be filled only during the same recess in which it arises.[102]

Summary

With respect to this particular phrase, Attorneys General since the early 20th century, as well as the Eleventh Circuit, have adopted the broader construction of "the Recess," finding it to be both consistent with the spirit of the Clause and necessary for the continuous and efficient operation of the government. The functionalist interpretation of this phrase has been supported for a significant period of time, and its development appears to have coincided with the increased number and length of intrasession recesses. As such, given the evolving scheduling practices of the Senate, the parameters of what constitutes a recess for purposes of the Recess Appointments Clause arguably have become less clear. For example, questions have arisen surrounding what it means for the Senate to be in session, and the minimum length of time, if any, of a recess. Under the *Noel Canning* decision, however, the President's recess appointment power would be limited to instances when a vacancy comes into being during "the Recess," that is, the period after which the Senate adjourns *sine die*. The meaning of "the Recess" is arguably more clear-cut under the D.C. Circuit's holding. However, its interpretation of both key phrases in the Recess Appointments Clause, as discussed below, would also have implications for the traditionally prevailing understanding of consecutive recess appointments, as well as recess appointments to positions occupied by holdover appointees and to newly established positions.

AUTHORITY AND TENURE OF RECESS APPOINTEES

As a fundamental matter, a recess appointee possesses the same legal authority as a confirmed appointee.[103] The commission of a recess appointee expires "at the End of [the Senate's] next Session," whereas the service of a confirmed appointee continues until the end of the statutory term or at the pleasure of the President, subject to the requirements laid out by Congress in creating the position.[104] When the Senate reconvenes after a recess during the same session, this is considered a continuation of the session and is not regarded as the "next Session" within the meaning of the Clause.[105]

COMPARISON OF LENGTH OF RECESS APPOINTMENTS

A comparison of two recess appointments during the 108th Congress illustrates the difference in recess appointment duration that results from the timing of appointments. During the intersession recess between the first and second sessions of the 108th Congress, President George W. Bush appointed Charles W. Pickering to a court of appeals judgeship. Several weeks later, during the first instrasession recess of the second session of the 108th Congress, President Bush appointed William H. Pryor Jr. to a judgeship on another court of appeals. Pickering's commission expired after less than 11 months, at the end of the second session of the 108th Congress, whereas Pryor's commission would have expired after approximately 22 months, at the end of the first session of the 109th Congress. Ultimately, Pryor was confirmed by the Senate before the end of his recess appointment commission. However, it is noteworthy that although the Pickering and Pryor recess appointments were only several weeks apart, Pryor would be able to serve nearly twice as long because his appointment was made during an intrasession recess.

In practice, this means that a recess appointment could last for almost two years. (See textbox.) On the one hand, if an individual receives an intersession recess appointment—that is, an appointment between sessions of the same or successive Congresses—such individual could serve until the end of the following session. On the other hand, if the President makes an intrasession recess appointment— that is, an appointment during a recess of the Senate in the middle of a session, like the traditional August recess of a first session of Congress—that appointment would expire at the end of the second session. In the latter case, the duration of the appointment will include the rest of the session in progress plus the full length of the session that follows.[106]

The President may remove a recess appointee before the expiration of his term, either by outright removal (assuming he otherwise has discretionary removal authority with respect to the office) or by having another nominee confirmed by the Senate.[107]

What Is the Tenure of a Recess Appointee Who Is Also the Nominee?

Oftentimes an individual given a recess appointment is also the President's nominee to the office. A question may arise as to how long a recess appointee may serve after being confirmed by the Senate to an office that has as a fixed statutory term. Such tenure would appear to depend on the particular statutory language regarding the terms of office and filling of vacancies, rather than any constitutional limitations. For example, Attorney General Homer Cummings in 1933 opined that the new commission for the full statutory term relates back to the date on which the person first assumed office by means of the recess appointment.[108] In this instance, the nomination submitted by the President and confirmed by the Senate stated that the individual was being nominated to serve as Surgeon General "for the period of four years beginning June 1, 1931," which was the date the recess appointment commenced.[109] While recognizing that earlier Attorneys General opinions (discussed *infra*) had concluded the opposite, Attorney General Cummings remarked that the "substantial question" is "what did Congress intend?" The Attorney General concluded that his interpretation for this position was supported by the fact that the "War Department, the President, and the Senate have ... acted upon a view that the prescribed 'period of four years' is four years of service, notwithstanding that a particular appointee may serve his four years partly under one appointment and partly under another," as well as evidence of this interpretation with respect to other appointments.[110]

On the other hand, other Attorneys General legal opinions have concluded that the term of office for a confirmed appointee should not include any previous period of service under a recess appointment. These conclusions relied on the Supreme Court's decision in *United States v. Kirkpatrick*, where the Court held that a new appointment made by the President, by and with the advice and consent of the Senate, once accepted by the individual "was a virtual superseding and surrender of the former commission," which was a recess appointment made pursuant to the statute at issue (as opposed to the President's constitutional reccss appointment power).[111] According to the Court, "the commissions are not only different in date, and given under different authorities ..., but they are of different natures. The first is limited in its duration to a specified period [i.e., to the end of the Senate's next session]; the second is unlimited in duration, and during the pleasure of the President."[112]

Attorney General John Berrien in 1830 later applied this rationale to other officers who had been appointed during a recess and subsequently confirmed by the Senate. He stated:

> [I]t seems very clear that an appointment of a navy agent, made in the case of a vacancy occurring during the recess, is in the exercise of the *constitutional* power of the President ...; and that the constitutional limitation of such appointment is to the end of the succeeding session of Congress, unless it be sooner determined by the acceptance of a new commission under an appointment made by and with the advice and consent of the Senate. In such a case, therefore, I apprehend that the four years prescribed by law as the official term of the appointee, must commence to run from the date of the new commission..." (emphasis in the original)[113]

Moreover, even if a recess appointee who is also the President's nominee is rejected by the Senate, this does not constitute a removal. The rejected nominee may still hold office pursuant to his recess appointment under the Constitution until the termination of the session.[114]

May the President Make Successive Recess Appointments?

Upon the expiration of the constitutional term of a recess appointee, a new recess appointment, either of the same, or another person, may be made.[115] Successive recess appointments of the same individual, however, may implicate certain statutory pay restrictions, discussed below. While there are no constitutional limits on how many times the President may exercise the recess appointment authority with a particular individual, notably, the court in

Staebler v. Carter stated that a President "could probably not consistently with the principle of checks and balances grant a recess appointment to one rejected for the particular position by a vote of the Senate."[116]

However, were the D.C. Circuit's interpretation of the Recess Appointments Clause to be adopted ultimately by the U.S. Supreme Court, it seems the President would not have the authority to make successive recess appointments. In *Noel Canning*, one of the three recess appointments challenged had been made to a position that was vacated by the departure of an outgoing recess appointee.[117] According to the court, a vacancy to the outgoing recess appointment did not arise because the Clause provides that a recess appointment expires "at the End of [the Senate's] next Session," not "at the beginning of the Senate's next Recess."[118] Based on the D.C. Circuit's interpretation of the Clause, the President would not be able to make a second recess appointment to the same position because the expiration of a recess appointment would become vacant before "the Recess" rather than arise during "the Recess." It appears that from the D.C. Circuit's perspective, the constitutional expiration of a recess appointment would never come within the limited set of circumstances identified by the court as permitting the President to exercise his recess appointment power.

When is There a Vacancy if There Is a Statutory Holdover Provision?

A vacancy must exist before the President can exercise his recess appointment authority.[119] While this observation may seem self-evident, what constitutes a "vacancy" for the purposes of the Recess Appointments Clause may be complicated by the presence of a "holdover" provision that regularly accompanies fixed term positions.[120] The Department of Justice has generally held the view that as a matter of constitutional law, there is a vacancy for purposes of the Recess Appointments Clause when an appointment for a fixed term expires and the officer continues serving under a holdover provision.[121] Judicial interpretation of whether a vacancy exists in light of a holdover provision has been uneven depending on the statute's language.

Judicial Interpretations

In *Staebler v. Carter*, the U.S. District Court for the District of Columbia (D.C. District Court) held that there was a vacancy for purposes of the Recess Appointments Clause when an incumbent commissioner at the Federal

Election Commission (FEC) continued to exercise his authority pursuant to a holdover provision.[122] The Federal Election Campaign Act's holdover provision stated: "A member of the Commission may serve ... after the expiration of his own term until his successor has taken office."[123] As such, a member could continue to serve indefinitely until replaced by a successor. The court upheld a recess appointment to the FEC that was still occupied by a holdover FEC commissioner, based on a determination that the expiration of the holdover commissioner's formal term created an immediate and ongoing vacancy.[124] The plaintiff in *Staebler* argued that the Recess Appointments Clause was designed to operate only when no person is available to occupy a particular office. Rejecting this argument, the court stated that it was not persuaded this was the intention of the Framers because under such an interpretation, "the President would be prohibited from making a recess appointment when a term of office has expired, as long as someone with a permissive claim to the office is still serving."[125] As part of its reasoning for finding that a vacancy existed once the statutory term of office expired, the court stated: "In the absence of clearly-expressed legislative intent, the [c]ourt will not speculate that the Congress sought to achieve a result which would be both unusual and probably beyond its constitutional power."[126]

Conversely, in *Mackie v. Clinton* the D.C. District Court held that there was no vacancy for purposes of the Recess Appointments Clause when interpreting the holdover provision for a member of the Board of Governors of the United States Postal Service.[127] The court in *Mackie* declared that whether a vacancy exists for Recess Appointments Clause purposes depends on the wording and structure of the particular holdover provision. Here, the relevant holdover provision states that a "Governor may continue to serve after the expiration of his term until his successor has qualified, but not to exceed one year."[128] In the court's view, this holdover provision, unlike that in *Staebler*, creates a "prospective vacancy,"[129] rather than an immediate vacancy, such that the Governor holding over would continue to occupy the office for one year past the end of his term unless he died, resigned, was lawfully removed, or some other successor qualified.[130] The court further emphasized that unlike the indefinite holdover period in the Federal Election Campaign Act, the one-year holdover period prevented this board from being susceptible to the concerns expressed by the court in *Staebler*.

The D.C. District Court reached a similar conclusion in *Wilkinson v. Legal Servs. Corp.*[131] It held that there was no vacancy upon the expiration of a term of office of one of the Directors at the Legal Services Corporation (LSC). Rather, a vacancy is created upon the "resignation, death or removal of one of the sitting Directors."[132] However, *Wilkinson* distinguished itself from *Staebler* and *Mackie* in finding the holdover provision in the LSC Act mandatory: "Each member of the Board *shall* continue to serve until the successor to such member has been appointed and qualified" (emphasis added). Although the court found that the LSC Act provided no definition of "vacancy" as in *Staebler* (see note 124), nor any time limit that a holdover may remain in office as in *Mackie*, it held that "the plain meaning of this [holdover] language is that each member of the Board remains a Director after that person's term has expired until the new Director has been 'appointed' by the President and 'qualified.'"[133] The *Wilkinson* court concluded that the holdover provision did not infringe upon the President's recess appointment power; "it merely defined when 'vacancies' exist on the LSC Board sufficient to trigger application of the Recess Appointments Clause."[134] The decisions in *Staebler*, *Mackie*, and *Wilkinson* demonstrate that the issue of whether a holdover provision constitutes a vacancy for recess appointment purposes may depend upon the specific language contained therein.[135]

Even though courts have generally recognized the President's ability to make a recess appointment to a position that is occupied by an individual serving in a holdover capacity, whether the position is considered vacant depends on the statutory language, as discussed above. However, the *Noel Canning* decision, if adopted, could also potentially affect the President's ability to make recess appointments under holdover circumstances regardless of the language of the holdover provision. Broadly speaking, the expiration of a term of office is equal to the beginning of a holdover period and therefore a vacancy for purposes of the recess appointments clause to which someone can be appointed. Yet, because *Noel Canning* provides that any vacancy that may be filled under the Clause would be limited to those which arise during "the Recess," the D.C. Circuit's holding in *Noel Canning* would arguably place a further limitation on the President's authority to replace a holdover using his recess appointment power, unless the expiration of a statutory term of office coincides with the Senate entering "the Recess," or adjourning *sine die*.

STATUTORY PAY RESTRICTIONS ON RECESS APPOINTEES

It should be noted that there exists a statutory framework that governs the filling of vacancies that falls outside the scope of the Recess Appointments Clause. Since the early history of the republic, Congress has established a statutory framework designed to protect the Senate's constitutional role in the confirmation process.[136] The Vacancies Act, which has legislative roots dating back to 1795 and was most recently amended in 1998, establishes which individuals may be designated by the President to temporarily perform the duties and functions of a vacant office and the length of time a designee may serve.[137]

Early Statutory Pay Restriction

Notwithstanding the provisions of the Vacancies Act, Congress, in an attempt to check the President's use of the Recess Appointment Clause and preserve its role in the appointments process, has enacted legislation that would restrict the pay of recess appointees. Pay restrictions on recess appointees have a long history dating back to the mid-19th century. The forerunner to current statutory provisions was an appropriations rider that Congress attached to the FY1864 Army Appropriations Act. Among other conditions, the rider prohibited the payment of money from the Treasury: "as a salary, to any person appointed during the recess of the Senate, to fill a vacancy in any existing office, which vacancy existed while the Senate was in session and is by law required to be filled by and with the advice and consent of the Senate, until such appointee shall have been confirmed by the Senate."[138]

Under this language, an officer might have to serve without pay, until such time as the Senate consented to the nomination. These pay restrictions were enacted in response to President Lincoln's recess appointments of hundreds of military officers in violation of statutory authorization.[139] Although the interpretation of "Vacancies that may happen" was still in flux, as discussed above, Senator William P. Fessenden, elaborating on the intent of the appropriations rider, stated: "It may not be in our power to prevent the appointment, but it is in our power to prevent the payment; and when payment is prevented, I think that will probably put an end to the habit of making such appointments."[140]

Further restrictions were placed on the President's appointment and removal powers with the passage of the Tenure of Office Act in 1867.[141]

- Section 2 of the act purported to limit the President's power to suspend officers during a recess to instances where it was determined to the satisfaction of the President that an officer was guilty of misconduct in office, crime, or was incapable or legally disqualified to hold office. Removals made during recesses were to be reported to the Senate after it reconvened; and, if the Senate did not concur with the suspension, the suspended officer was to "resume the functions of his office."[142]

- Section 3 of the act purported to limit the President's authority to make recess appointments, providing that such an appointment could be made only if the vacancy occurred by death or resignation. If a recess appointee's nomination was not thereafter confirmed in the next session of the Senate, the office was to "remain in abeyance."[143]

The act also delineated criminal penalties and cut-off of salary for violations of its provisions. President Andrew Johnson, who believed the act to unconstitutionally infringe upon the power of the executive, ignored the provisions of the act when he removed Secretary of War Edwin Stanton from office, undoubtedly precipitating Johnson's impeachment.[144] Congress repealed part of the act in 1869[145] and then entirely in 1887.[146] Though the act was not challenged in the courts, similar limits on the President's removal power were struck down as unconstitutional in the 1926 decision of *Myers v. United States*.[147]

Modern Statutory Pay Restriction (5 U.S.C. §5503)

Even though these types of congressional restrictions on the President's removal powers have been held unconstitutional, the pay restriction for recess appointees that was originally enacted in 1863 remained intact until it was amended in 1940 to provide exceptions to the flat prohibition, making it less burdensome on officeholders. The pay restriction on recess appointees is currently codified at 5 U.S.C. §5503.[148]

The second exception—(a)(2)—which allows a recess appointee to be paid, so long as there is a pending nomination before the Senate that is not of a person who had been appointed during the preceding recess, has implied preclusive effect. Generally, subsection (a)(2) has been interpreted as prohibiting the payment of compensation to successive recess appointees.[150] However, looking more closely at the text, it has also been observed that (a)(2) prohibits payment to a successive recess appointee "*only* where the person receiving the recess appointment was already serving under a prior recess appointment. ... Thus, if someone *other than* a prior recess appointee whose nomination was pending at the time of adjournment is appointed, §5503(a)(2) does not bar payment."[151] Given this observation, it is conceivable that the same individual could be recess appointed a second time and paid under (a)(2), so long as there is a different individual whose nomination is pending for the position.[152]

DESCRIPTION OF 5 U.S.C. §5503(A)

This statute generally provides that an individual who is given a recess appointment to fill a vacancy in an existing office *may not* receive payment from the Treasury of the United States[149] if the vacancy existed while the Senate was in session and was by law required to be filled by and with the advice and consent of the Senate.

Such an individual can receive pay once he has been confirmed by the Senate. However, there are three exceptions under which a recess appointee *may be paid*:

- (a)(1)- if the vacancy arose within 30 days before the end of the session;
- (a)(2)- if, at the end of the session, a nomination for the office, other than the nomination of an individual appointed during the preceding recess, [is] pending before the Senate for its advice and consent; or
- (a)(3)- if a pending nomination was rejected 30 days before the session ended and an individual, other than the one whose nomination was rejected, is given the recess appointment.

Overall, while §5503(a)(2) implicitly bars payments to successive recess appointees, a closer reading of the text could suggest the prohibition to be narrow, and in fact allow payment to a successive recess appointee, depending on the individuals who are recess appointed and nominated to the position.[153]

If a recess appointee is paid under one of the three exceptions, then §5503(b) provides that a nomination to fill a vacancy must be submitted to the Senate not later than 40 days after the beginning of the next session of the Senate. For this reason, when a recess appointment is made, the President generally submits a new nomination to the position even when an old nomination is pending. Although an individual whose nomination has been rejected may continue to serve until the commission expires, another long-standing appropriations rider that reinforces the third exception under §5503 prevents any payment to an individual to fill a position "for which he or she has been nominated after the Senate has voted not to approve the nomination of said person."[154]

The three exceptions under §5503 which would allow payment, were designed, as stated in a House report, "to render the existing prohibition on the payment of salaries more flexible."[155] The report further explained that

> [f]rom a practical standpoint it frequently creates difficulties especially in those cases in which a vacancy arose shortly before the close of a congressional session, leaving insufficient time to fill the vacancy by nomination and confirmation. Difficulties also arise in cases in which a session terminates before the Senate acts on pending nominations, as has at times happened.[156]

Unlike the Recess Appointments Clause where the term "Session" indicates the adjournment *sine die* of the Senate, the term "session" for purposes of §5503 refers to any time the Senate convenes. The version of this law preceding §5503 used the phrase "termination of the session" as opposed to the phrase "end of the session," which now appears in §5503(a)(1). This revision was not intended as a substantive change, however. The "termination" phrase was interpreted by the Comptroller General to encompass "any adjournment, whether final or not, in contemplation of a recess covering a substantial period of time."[157]

Anti-Deficiency Act and Voluntary Services

Sometimes it has been argued that a recess appointee, who is generally barred from receiving pay unless one of the three exceptions applies, would be then barred from serving because of a provision of the Anti-Deficiency Act, namely 31 U.S.C. §1342.[158] This provision states, "An officer or employee of the United States government or of the District of Columbia government may not accept voluntary services for either government or employ personal services exceeding that authorized by law except for emergencies involving the safety of human life or the protection of property."[159]

Because the voluntary services prohibition is designed to prevent federal agencies from seeking additional appropriations,[160] interpretations of 31 U.S.C. §1342 have concluded that although the section prohibits federal entities from accepting voluntary services, it does not prohibit acceptance of gratuitous services for which no future claim for compensation will be made.[161] Pursuant to this distinction, the Government Accountability Office (GAO) has ruled that compensation that is not fixed by statute may be waived, so long as the waiver renders any service gratuitous. Conversely, GAO has ruled that compensation that is fixed by statute may not be waived and deemed gratuitous without specific statutory authority.[162]

While 31 U.S.C. §1342 may be controlling with regard to prohibiting officers and employees from accepting voluntary services, there does not appear to be any basis for its application to recess appointees, who are statutorily barred from receiving pay under 5 U.S.C. §5503, regardless of whether the position at issue carries a discretionary or fixed rate of pay. In other words, it does not seem that §1342, which prevents the government from accepting voluntary services from officers and employees, would also prevent recess appointees, who are already statutorily barred from receiving pay, from serving in government. Because the President's appointment power, including the power to make recess appointments, arises from the Constitution, it is difficult to formulate a rationale that would support the conclusion that a congressional enactment may prevent the service of a recess appointee who is already prevented from receiving pay, as the pay proscription itself clearly contemplates that recess appointees falling within its purview would continue to serve, further obviating the application of §1342.[163]

Do Pay Restrictions Raise Constitutional Concerns?

These pay limitations are designed to protect the Senate's advice and consent function. By targeting the compensation of appointees as opposed to the President's recess appointment power itself, the limitations act as indirect controls on recess appointments, and their constitutionality has not been adjudicated. However, the court in *Staebler* commented that "if any and all restrictions on the President's recess appointment power, however limited, are prohibited by the Constitution, 5 U.S.C. §5503 ... might also be invalid."[164] Additional constitutional concerns might arise from the application of these statutory restrictions to judicial recess appointees,[165] though Attorneys General have consistently advised Presidents of the applicability of the pay restriction statutes without raising constitutional concerns.[166]

The concerns raised in *Staebler*, which questioned the constitutionality of the restrictions with regard to recess appointments, coupled with the scope of the decision in *Evans v. Stephens*, could be seen as arguably giving rise to an expansive interpretation of the President's power under the Recess Appointments Clause. As touched upon above, the Eleventh Circuit in *Evans* upheld the intrasession recess appointment of William H. Pryor Jr. to that court, based upon a broad interpretation of the President's authority under the Clause. The majority's acceptance of brief intrasession recess appointments, together with the potential constitutional invalidity of the statutory restrictions, could lead to a dynamic whereby the President would have a legal and constitutional basis upon which to completely bypass the Senate confirmation process, in that the President would be empowered to make successive recess appointments during short recesses with the practical effect of enabling an appointee to serve throughout the course of an Administration without submitting to the Senate confirmation process.

Recognizing this, Judge Barkett, in a dissenting opinion, argued that a literal and restrictive interpretation of the Clause was necessitated by the "real, concrete concern that the understanding of the recess appointment power embraced by the majority will allow the President to repeatedly bypass the role the Framers intended the Senate to play in reviewing presidential nominees."[167] The D.C. Circuit in *Noel Canning* similarly recognized this possibility with respect to a broad interpretation of the Clause when it made its interpretation of the constitutional provision along more narrow parameters.[168] The decisions in *Staebler* and *Evans*, in contrast with *Noel Canning*, could arguably transform the Recess Appointments Clause from the supplementary and auxiliary mechanism, discussed by Alexander Hamilton, into a more significant grant of presidential power.

Congressional Efforts to Deter Recess Appointments

As previously discussed, as intrasession recesses became more common, it has been suggested that such a recess must be of an appropriate duration in order for the President to exercise his recess appointment authority. For instance, a position advanced by the Department of Justice through court briefs has suggested that the President may make recess appointments during any recess of the Senate in excess of three days.[169] Based on this understanding, the Senate, in recent years, has employed procedures for the purpose of preventing the President from making recess appointments.

CONGRESSIONAL RESOLUTIONS

Over time, Congress also has expressed disapproval of the President's use of his recess appointment authority. For example, resolutions objecting to Madison's appointments of envoys to Great Britain were debated in 1814, but not brought to a vote.[173] More recently, a "sense of the Senate" resolution enacted in 1960 expressing reservation over several recess appointments to the Supreme Court has arguably influenced presidential exercise of the recess appointment power in the judicial context.[174] Prompted by President Dwight D. Eisenhower's recess appointments of Earl Warren, William J. Brennan Jr., and Potter Stewart to the Supreme Court in 1953, 1956, and 1958, respectively, Senator Philip Hart introduced S.Res. 334 to discourage such appointments.[175] No recess appointments to the Supreme Court have been made since the enactment of this resolution, and there has been an attendant decrease in the number of judicial recess appointments generally, with only four such appointments occurring since 1960. The use of the recess appointment power in the judicial context remains a contentious issue in both the political and judicial spheres, as indicated by the 2004 decision in *Evans.*

Specifically, it has held several *pro forma* sessions, which are "brief meeting[s] (sometimes only several seconds) of the Senate in which no business is conducted. [They are] usually held to satisfy the constitutional obligation that neither chamber can adjourn for more than three days without the consent of the other."[170] For example, on November 16, 2007, Senate Majority Leader Harry Reid announced that the Senate would "be coming in for *pro forma* sessions during the Thanksgiving holiday to prevent recess appointments."[171] The Senate recessed later that day, and *pro forma* meetings were convened on November 20, 23, 27, and 29, with no business conducted. The Senate next conducted business after reconvening on December 3, 2007. Similar procedures were followed during the remainder of President Bush's term, and many perceived that this limited the ability of the President to make recess appointments during those periods.[172] During the 111th Congress, the Senate used these procedures during the latter part of the second session.

It structured its 2010 pre-election break as a series of shorter recesses separated by *pro forma* sessions. The use of this approach during two successive Congresses suggests that it has become regarded as an ongoing tool available to the Senate. During the 112th Congress, a letter to the Speaker of the House from 20 Senators urged the Speaker "to refuse to pass any resolution to allow the Senate to recess or adjourn for more than three days for the remainder of the president's term," and referred to the Senate practices of 2007 as a "successful attempt to thwart President Bush's recess appointment power."[176]

Congressional Scheduling Practice and the January 2012 Recess Appointments

The second session of the 112th Congress began at noon on January 3, 2012, as required by the Constitution.[177] This opening session was a *pro forma* session. When the House and Senate concluded their business at the end of the first session of the 112th Congress, no concurrent resolution of adjournment had been introduced or adopted. Rather, the Senate, by unanimous consent, agreed to reconvene on January 23, 2012. They further agreed to hold *pro forma* sessions during the interim period, with the apparent expectation that this would continue to block the President's ability to make a recess appointment.[178] On January 4, 2012, President Obama made four recess appointments—one to be director of the newly created Consumer Financial Protection Bureau (CFPB), and three to be members of the National Labor Relations Board (NLRB)— despite the Senate's use of *pro forma* sessions and lack of adjournment under the Adjournment Clause.[179]

The President's action was seen by some as controversial and interested parties have instituted a variety of legal proceedings to challenge the validity of these recess appointments.[180] As discussed above, the D.C. Circuit held in *Noel Canning* that the NLRB appointments violated the Recess Appointments Clause.[181] The court did not address any of the Attorneys General opinions from the 19th century that opted for a broader interpretation of the Recess Appointments Clause (as discussed in this report), nor the development or use of *pro forma* sessions to determine if the Senate is in a session or in a recess. While likely influential, this federal appellate decision appears limited to its jurisdiction and seems applicable only to the NLRB appointments. Post- *Noel Canning*, other federal courts of appeals have also issued decisions regarding the constitutionality of the President's recess appointments to the NLRB.[182] On June 24, 2013, the Supreme Court granted *certiorari* to review the *Noel Canning* decision.[183] The questions presented to the Court are:

1. Whether the President's recess appointment power may be exercised during a recess that occurs within a session of the Senate, or is instead limited to recesses that occur between enumerated sessions of the Senate;
2. Whether the President's recess appointment power may be exercised to fill vacancies that exist during a recess, or is instead limited to vacancies that first arose during that recess; and
3. Whether the President's recess appointment power may be exercised when the Senate is convening every three days in *pro forma* sessions.

Notably, the *Noel Canning* decision did not address other salient issues that were raised by the January 4, 2012, recess appointments. As such, the Supreme Court may examine the phrase "the Recess of the Senate" differently from the D.C. Circuit, and give consideration to the evolution of congressional scheduling and its effect on recess appointment practices, as well as the 19th century Attorneys General opinions and congressional committee reports. For example, as it pertains to intrasession recess appointments, the Court may choose to analyze what would be a sufficient number of days the Senate must be recessed for there to be a "Recess of the Senate." Is there a basis for linking the Adjournment Clause, which speaks to breaks of more than three days "during the Session of Congress," to the meaning of "recess" within the context of the Recess Appointments Clause, as advanced by the Department of Justice in its 1993 court brief?[184] Or, if there is no such basis, what criteria should be used to determine what constitutes a "recess" for purposes of the Recess Appointments Clause? With respect to the use of *pro forma* sessions, the Court may likely analyze whether the Senate is effectively in a "recess" when no business is conducted. Interestingly, the Department of Justice's opinion on the January 4, 2012, recess appointments emphasized a point from the 1921 Attorney General Daugherty opinion, where he opined that "I think the President is necessarily vested with a large, although not unlimited, discretion to determine when there is a real and genuine recess making it impossible for him to receive the advice and consent of the Senate."[185] This statement appears to highlight the new tension regarding which branch—the executive or the legislative—can trigger the conditions which permit the President to make a recess appointment. As this legislative practice is designed to prevent the President from exercising his constitutional authority to make recess appointments during periods when the Senate is not meeting, the Supreme Court may also need to determine whether this congressional practice could be taken to violate separation of powers principles.

CONCLUSION

While generally perceived as a straightforward, pragmatic provision designed to foster administrative continuity, the history of the Recess Appointments Clause shows that it also has been employed by Presidents for tactical and political purposes throughout the history of the republic. As such, the Clause has been the source of recurrent controversy, beginning with the Administration of George Washington, and continuing to the current Administration of Barack Obama. Historical interpretation and judicial treatment of the Clause have fleshed out many of its inherent ambiguities, to the extent that there is now precedent to support the propriety of recess appointments regardless of when the vacancy at issue arose, and to support such appointments during both intersession and intrasession recesses. However, many tensions remain regarding the proper scope and application of the Clause, especially in light of evolving congressional practices meant to block the President's ability to exercise his recess appointment authority. These tensions, coupled with the lack of any definitive consideration by the Supreme Court, would thus seem to ensure that the Clause will be a continuing source of political and legal controversy.

End Notes

[1] U.S. Const., art. II, §2, cl. 2. The appointment of other, so-called "inferior officers," may be vested by Congress in the President alone, courts, or the heads of departments. *Id.*

[2] U.S. Const., art. II, §2, cl. 3.

[3] CRS Report RS21308, *Recess Appointments: Frequently Asked Questions*, by Henry B. Hogue.

[4] *The Federalist, No. 67*, at 409-10 (Alexander Hamilton) (Clinton Rossiter ed. 1961).

[5] 2 *The Documentary History of the Ratification of the Constitution* 537 (Merrill Jensen, ed. 1976).

[6] Edward A. Hartnett, *Recess Appointments of Article III Judges: Three Constitutional Questions*, 26 Cardozo L. Rev. 377, 380-81 (2005) (quoting 4 *The Founders' Constitution* 37, 102-03 (P. Kurland ed., 1787)).

[7] *See* Michael B. Rappaport, *The Original Meaning of the Recess Appointments Clause*, 52 UCLA L. Rev. 1487, 1500- 01 (2005).

[8] Noel Canning v. Nat'l Labor Relations Bd., 705 F.3d 490 (D.C. Cir. 2013). *See also* Nat'l Labor Relations Bd. v. New Vista Nursing and Rehabilitation, No. 11-3440, 2013 U.S. App. LEXIS 9860 (3d Cir. May 16, 2013) (holding the recess appointment of Craig Becker to be a Member of the National Labor Relations Board during an intrasession recess unconstitutional and that the President's recess appointments power only extends to intersession recesses of the Senate); Nat'l Labor Relations Bd. v. Enter. Leasing Co. SE, No. 12-1514, 2013 U.S. App. LEXIS 14444 (4th Cir. Jul. 17, 2013) (holding that the three January 4, 2012, recess appointments are constitutionally infirm because they were not made during "the Recess of the Senate").

[9] Nat'l Labor Relations Bd. v. Noel Canning, No. 12-1281, 2013 U.S. LEXIS 4876 (Jun. 24, 2013).

[10] *See also* CRS Report R43032, *Practical Implications of Noel Canning on the NLRB and CFPB*, by David H. Carpenter and Todd Garvey, and CRS Report R43030, *The Recess Appointment Power After Noel Canning v. NLRB: Constitutional Implications*, by Todd Garvey and David H. Carpenter.

[11] *Id. See also* Michael A. Carrier, *When is the Senate in Recess for Purposes of the Recess Appointments Clause?*, 92 Mich. L. Rev. 2204, 2212 (1994).

[12] An intrasession recess refers to a recess of the Senate during a session of the Senate.

[13] Carrier, *supra* note 11, at 2212. Before the passage of the Twentieth Amendment in 1933, "the term of each Congress began on March 4th of each odd numbered year.... The Congress ... convened regularly on the first Monday in December. ... So, prior to 1934, a new Congress typically would not convene for regular business until 13 months after being elected." *Congressional Directory* at 526 (2009).

[14] Rappaport, *supra* note 7.

[15] *See* Nomination of Sitting Member of Congress to Ambassador to Vietnam, 20 Op. Off. Legal Counsel 284, 289 (1996).

[16] *See* Fish, Carl R., *Removal of Officials by the Presidents of the United States*, Annual Report of the American Historical Association for the Year 1899. Vol. 1. Washington, D.C., Government Printing Office (1900).

[17] Thomas A Curtis, *Recess Appointments to Article III Courts: The Use of Historical Practice in Constitutional Interpretation*, 84 Colum. L. Rev. 1758, 1755 (1984).

[18] *Id.* at 1775-76.

[19] *Id.* at 1776.

[20] Henry B. Hogue, *The Law: Recess Appointments to Article III Courts*, Presidential Studies Quarterly 34, No. 3 at 661 (2004).

[21] A spoils system refers to a system of patronage, in which the winning political party will give government jobs to its supporters who worked toward the victory as opposed to awarding offices on the basis of some measure of merit, independent from any political activity.

[22] *See infra* "Statutory Pay Restrictions on Recess Appointees" and note 139 and accompanying text.

[23] *See infra* "Statutory Pay Restrictions on Recess Appointees" and note 143 and accompanying text.

[24] *See* Curtis, *supra* note 17, at 1758.

[25] The potential effect of this decision on the specific appointments and agency at issue is beyond the scope of this report.

[26] Edmund Randolph, *Opinion on Recess Appointments* (July 7, 1792), in 24 The Papers of Thomas Jefferson, at 165- 67 (John Catanzariti et al., ed., 1990) (Attorney General Randolph was responding to an inquiry from Thomas Jefferson, then serving as Secretary of Foreign Affairs). *See also*, Hartnett, *supra* note 6, at 384-86; Rappaport, *supra* note 7, at 1518-19.

[27] Randolph, *supra* note 26 , at 166; Rappaport, *supra* note 7, at 1519.

[28] *Id.*

[29] Rappaport, *supra* note 7, at 1519. The "special law" to which Hamilton refers is a law that would vest the appointment of an "inferior Officer" in the President alone. Under such a law, Congress could allow the President alone to make "a permanent appointment of an inferior officer, or a temporary appointment extending till the end of the next session, irrespective of when the vacancy arose." *Id.* at n.92.

[30] Executive Authority to Fill Vacancies, 1 Op. Att'y Gen. 631, 633-34 (1823).

[31] *Id.*

[32] *Id.* at 632.

[33] *See* George H. Haynes, *The Senate of the United States*, Vol. 2 at 772-75 (Russell and Russell ed., 1960). In 1814, Senator Christopher Gore insisted "[i]f a vacancy happen in an office,

the office must have been before full.... If a vacancy exist prior to, it does not happen in the recess of the Senate." 26 Annals of Congress 654 (March 7, 1814). In contrast, his contemporary, Senator George Bibb, "den[ied] that the word 'vacancy,' in its usual application or in its application to office, implies a previous filling.... A vacant office is 'an office unoccupied,' 'an office not filled.'" 26 Annals of Congress 697-98 (March 30, 1814); *see id.* at 742-59 (April 12, 1814). In 1863, Senator Jacob Howard issued a report from the Senate Committee on the Judiciary examining recess appointments. He agreed with Senator Gore from 40 years earlier, that a "President might not appoint to fill vacancies which 'have not occurred within the recess of the Senate.'" S.Rept. 37-80, at 3 (37th Cong., 3d sess. 1863).

[34] 3 *Joseph Story, Commentaries on the Constitution on the United States*, §1553 (Boston, Hillard, Gray & Co. 1833) ("If the senate are in session when offices are created by law, which have not as yet been filled, and nominations are not then made to them by the president, he cannot appoint to such offices during the recess of the senate, because the vacancy does not happen during the recess of the senate."). Senator Littleton Tazewell made speeches where he repeatedly argued that "the President alone has no authority to make an original appointment to a statutory office." 7 Reg. Deb. 225 (February 22, 1831); *see also* 2 Reg. Deb. 607 (April 20, 1826) ("In relation to statutory offices of every kind, however, it has never been pretended by anyone ... that the President might make an original appointment to them. They have always been filled, for the first time, by and with the advice and consent of the Senate ...").

[35] Power of the President to Fill Vacancies, 2 Op. Att'y Gen. 525, 526 (1832) (supporting an expansive definition of "Vacancies that may happen," but also noting that "[t]he appointment ... during the last recess 'filled up' the vacancy which had happened, and the office remained full; and there was no vacancy, from the time of his appointment and acceptance until the close of the late session. The nomination made not being confirmed by the Senate, the commission granted by the President expired at the end of the session; and the moment after it closed, the office again became vacant. This was a new vacancy."); Power of President to Fill Vacancies, 3 Op. Att'y Gen. 673, 676 (1841) ("My opinion is, that the same overruling necessity which applied to the original vacancy applies to the second one, created by an omission of the Senate to act on a nomination.").

[36] 2 Op. Att'y Gen. *supra* note 35, at 526-27.

[37] *Id.* at 528 (emphasis in original).

[38] Appointment of Judges, &c (etc.), for Iowa and Florida, 4 Op. Att'y Gen. 361, 363 (1845). However, an 1868 Attorney General opinion indicated that a subsequent opinion issued by Attorney General Mason regarding "his views of the President's power to grant temporary commissions, in the recess of the Senate, were subsequently quite different from those indicated in the opinion on the case of the federal officers in Florida and Iowa; for in the later opinion, he expresses his general concurrence in the construction of the constitutional provision under consideration adopted by his predecessors." *See* Case of the Collectorship of Customs in Alaska, 12 Op. Att'y Gen. 455, 456 (1868).

[39] Power of the President to Appoint to Office During Recess of the Senate, 4 Op. Att'y Gen. 523, 525 (1846).

[40] S.Rept. 37-80 (37th Cong., 3d Sess. 1863).

[41] Ambassadors and Other Public Ministers of the United States Opinion,7 Op. Att'y Gen. 186 (1855); Filling Vacancies in Office, 18 Op. Att'y Gen. 28 (1884); Vacancy in Office, 19 Op. Att'y Gen. 261 (1889).

[42] President's Appointing Power, 10 Op. Att'y Gen. 356 (1862).

[43] President's Power to Fill Vacancies in Recess of the Senate, 12 Op. Att'y Gen. 32, 34 (1866) (emphasis in original).

[44] *Id.* at 38.

[45] Case of the Collectorship of New Orleans, 12 Op. Att'y Gen. 449, 452 (1868). Attorney General Evarts concluded that "upon the well-considered and long-continued interpretation

of [the Recess Appointments Clause] ..., the President has the power to fill the vacancy in the office of collector at New Orleans, by granting a commission that shall expire at the end of the next session of the Senate, and that the "tenure-of-civil-office act" does not in terms, nor intent, nor in the legislative construction of this clause ..., affect this power of the President." *Id.* at 454. Evarts also considered the merits of the opposing interpretation, in light of legislation considered by Congress, but ultimately concluding that he could not but concur with "the views of [his] learned predecessors." *Id.* at 452.

[46] *See* Temporary Appointments in the Army,14 Op. Att'y Gen. 562 (1875); Temporary Appointments by the President, 15 Op. Att'y Gen. 207 (1877); Appointments During Recess of the Senate, 16 Op. Att'y Gen. 522 (1880); District Attorney-Temporary Appointment, 16 Op. Att'y Gen. 538 (1880); Appointments to Office, 17 Op. Att'y Gen. 521 (1883); Vacancies in Office, 18 Op. Att'y Gen. 29 (1884); Vacancy in Office, 19 Op. Att'y Gen. 261 (1889); President- Recess Appointment-Naval Officer, 26 Op. Att'y Gen. 234 (1907); President-Recess Appointment-Post Master, 30 Op. Att'y Gen. 314 (1914); Executive Power-Recess Appointments, 33 Op. Att'y Gen. 20 (1921); Recess Appointments, 41 Op. Att'y Gen. 463 (1960); Recess Appointments Issues, 6 U.S. Op. Off. Legal Counsel 585 (1982).

[47] 12 Stat. 642, 646 (1863). The appropriations rider also provided that no money was to be paid from the Treasury "to any person acting or assuming to act as an officer, civil, military, or naval, as salary in any office, which is not authorized by some previously existing law, unless where such office shall be subsequently sanctioned by law." *Id.*

[48] Rev. Stat. §1761, ch.580, 54 Stat. 751 (1940), codified at 5 U.S.C. §56 (1940).

[49] *In re* Farrow, 3 Fed. 112, 116 (C.C.N.D. Ga. 1880) (stating that the President has the power to make appointments "notwithstanding the fact that the vacancy filled by his appointment first happened when the [S]enate was in session.").

[50] *Id.* at 115.

[51] *Id.* at 115 (rejecting the holding in *Case of District Attorney of United States*, 7 Fed. Cas. 731 (No. 3,924, E.D. Pa. 1868)); *see also*, contrary opinion in *Schenck v. Peay*, 21 Fed. Cas. 672 (No. 12,451 E.D. Ark. 1869).

[52] *In re* Yancey, 28 Fed. 445, 450 (C.C.W.D. Tenn. 1886) (holding the recess appointment of a marshal by the President to be lawful, and that there was no need to turn to other legal mechanisms to qualify the appointment).

[53] United States v. Allocco, 305 F.3d 704, 712 (2d Cir. 1962), *cert. denied*, 371 U.S. 964 (1963) (holding President Eisenhower's appointment of John M. Cashin to a federal judgeship during an intersession recess valid).

[54] United States v. Woodley, 751 F.2d 1008, 1012 (9th Cir. 1985), *cert. denied*, 475 U.S. 1048 (1986) (holding President Carter's appointment of Walter Heen to a federal judgeship during an intersession recess valid).

[55] Evans v. Stephens, 387 F.3d 1220, 1226-27 (11th Cir. 2004), *cert. denied*, 544 U.S. 942 (2005) (holding President Bush's appointment of William H. Pryor Jr. to a federal judgeship during an intrasession recess valid). The decisions in *Allocco, Woodley*, and *Evans* are additionally significant, in that all three held that the President's power under the Recess Appointments Clause extends to filling judicial vacancies on Article III courts. For an analysis of the interplay of the Recess Appointments Clause and Article III of the Constitution, *see* CRS Report RL32971, *Judicial Recess Appointments: A Legal Overview*, by T. J. Halstead.

[56] *See, e.g., Allocco*, 305 F.3d at 713 (citing *Youngstown Sheet and Tube v. Sawyer*, 343 U.S. 579 (1952), the court concluded that "a systematic, unbroken, executive practice, long pursued to the knowledge of the Congress and never before questioned ... may be treated as a gloss on the 'Executive Power' vested in the President." *Id.*).

[57] *Noel Canning*, 705 F.3d at 507.

[58] *Id.* at 512.

[59] *Id.* at 507.

[60] *Id.* ("Dictionaries at the time of the Constitution defined "happen" as "[t]o fall out; to chance; to come to pass. [citations omitted]" *Id.*).

[61] U.S. Const., art. I., §3, cl. 2. The Seventeenth Amendment, ratified in 1913, modified this clause when it allowed the executive authority of a state to make temporary appointments, provided that "the legislature of any State may empower the executive thereof to make temporary appointments until the people fill the vacancies by election as the legislature may direct." U.S. Const., amend XVII.

[62] *Noel Canning*, 705 F.3d at 508.

[63] *Id.*

[64] *Id.* at 511. ("The power of a written constitution lies in its words. It is those words that were adopted by the people. When those words speak clearly, it is not up to us to depart from their meaning in favor of our own concept of efficiency, convenience, or facilitation of the functions of government." *Id.* at 511-12.).

[65] *Id.* at 510 (citing *United States v. Chadha*, 462 U.S. 919, 942, n.13 (1983), "The assent of the Executive to a bill which contains a provision contrary to the Constitution does not shield it from judicial review.").

[66] *See infra* "Statutory Pay Restrictions on Recess Appointees."

[67] *Farrow*, 3 Fed. at 115.

[68] *See* Carrier, *supra* note 11, at 2212-13.

[69] President-Appointment of Officers-Holiday Recess, 23 Op. Att'y Gen. 599 (1901).

[70] *Id.* at 600 (emphasis in original).

[71] *Id.* at 603.

[72] *See* Gould v. United States, 19 Ct. Cl. 593 (1884) (holding "we have no doubt that a vacancy occurring while the Senate was thus temporarily adjourned, from July 20 to November 21, 1867, could be legally filled by appointment of the President alone ..." *Id.* at 595-96.).

[73] Executive Power-Recess Appointments, 33 Op. Att'y Gen. 20, 23 (1921).

[74] *Id.* at 23.

[75] S.Rept. 58-4389, at 2 (58th Cong. 3d sess., 1905) (emphasis in the original); 39 Cong. Rec. 3823-24 (1905).

[76] 33 Op. Att'y Gen., *supra* note 73, at 25.

[77] *Id.* at 25.

[78] 37 Cong. Rec. 544 (December 7, 1905) ("Final Adjournment—The hour of 12 o'clock having arrived, the President pro tempore said: Senators, the hour provided by law for the meeting of the first regular session of the Fifty-eighth Congress having arrived, I declare the extraordinary session adjourned without day."). Prior to the adoption of the Twentieth Amendment to the Constitution in 1933, the term of Congress began on March 4 of each odd-numbered year. The new Congress, however, typically convened for the first time on the first Monday of the following December and adjourned in the spring of the following year. U.S. Const. art. I, §4, cl. 2. The second session would typically convene on the following first Monday of December in the even-numbered year, and continue until no later than March 3 of the following year, the day prior to the beginning of the next Congress. Pre-1933, the term of a newly elected President also began on March 4. Accordingly, the President sometimes would call the Senate into "special" session on or shortly after March 4, or call both Houses into an "extraordinary" session before the constitutionally set date. For more information *see* CRS Congressional Distribution Memorandum, "Recess Appointments During Short Intervals Between Sessions and Historical Efforts to Prevent Recess Appointments through Congressional Scheduling," by Henry Hogue and Richard Beth (June 8, 2012) [hereinafter Hogue/Beth CDM].

[79] Many of these officers had been granted a recess appointment during the prior recess, and most, but not all, had been confirmed. For those officers not yet confirmed, the Administration wished to "avoid, if possible, the legal complications and questions which would result from throwing [the unconfirmed] officers back into the positions from which

they had been promoted, or possibly excluding them altogether from office in the Army." *See* "Recess Appointments," 38 Cong. Rec. 1604 (1904).

[80] *See* Hogue/Beth CDM, *supra* note 78, at 14-20. Roosevelt's actions could be viewed as a practical manifestation of the potential infirmities of the Knox interpretation; that is, if a formalistic interpretation of the Clause rests upon a concern that allowing intrasession appointments will foster systematic avoidance of the Senate's advice and consent function, the fact that a President is able to make such appointments during an instantaneous "constructive recess" of the Senate would appear to belie such a distinction. *See also* Hartnett, *supra* note 6, at 416.

[81] It appears that none of the recess appointments made during this "constructive" recess were invalidated. Each of the officers who had been given a recess appointment was nominated by the President on the following day, December 8, 1903, to the position to which he had been recess appointed. The most controversial nominee, that of Leonard Wood to be a major general in the U.S. Army, was confirmed on March 18, 1904, while the remaining military officer nominees were confirmed a few days later on March 22. *See* U.S. Congress, Senate, *Journal of the Executive Proceedings of the Senate of the United States of America*, vol. XXXV at 101-109.

[82] *See, e.g.*, Recess Appointments During an Intrasession Recess, 16 Op. Off. Legal Counsel 15 (1992) (explaining that Attorney General Daugherty noted that the "line of demarcation cannot be accurately drawn," and "[t]he longstanding view of the Attorneys General has been that the term 'recess' includes intrasession recesses if they are substantial in length" *Id.* at 15-16.); Intrasession Recess Appointments, 13 Op. Off. Legal Counsel 271 (1989); Recess Appointments Issues, 6 Op. Off. Legal Counsel 585 (1982); Recess Appointments, 41 Op. Att'y Gen. 463 (1960).

[83] *See, e.g.*, Memorandum of Points and Authorities in Support of Defendants' Opposition to Plaintiffs' Motion for Partial Summary Judgment, at 24-6, Mackie v. Clinton, 827 F. Supp. 56 (D.D.C. 1993), *vacated as moot*, 10 F.3d 13 (D.C. Cir. 1993) [hereinafter DOJ Brief] (arguing that the President may be able to make a recess appointment during a recess of more than three days because constitutionally, neither chamber can adjourn for more than three days without the consent of the other pursuant to the Adjournments Clause, implying that the Framers did not consider one, two, or three day recesses to be constitutionally significant); Brief for the United States in Opposition to Petition for *Writ of Certiorari*, at 11, Evans v. Stephens, 387 F.3d 1220 (11th Cir. 2004), *cert. denied*, 544 U.S. 942 (2005); and Transcript of Oral Argument at 50, New Process Steele v. Nat'l Labor Relations Bd., 130 S. Ct. 2635 (2010).

[84] Kennedy v. Sampson, 511 F.2d 430 (D.C. Cir. 1974).

[85] U.S. Const., art. I, §7, cl. 2.

[86] *See* Barnes v. Kline, 759 F.2d 21 (D.C. Cir. 1985) (invalidating intersession pocket veto), *vacated as moot sub nom.*, Burke v. Barnes, 479 U.S. 361 (1987).

[87] Constitutional Law-Article II, Section 2, Clause 3- Recess Appointments-Compensation (5 U.S.C. 5503), 3 Op. Off. Legal Counsel 314, 316 (1979).

[88] The number of days adjourned is counted starting on the first calendar day after an adjournment and ending on the day of reconvening, including in the count the day of the day the Senate reconvened. This is consistent with the House practice for counting recess days for purposes of meeting congressional adjournment requirements in the Constitution. 808472219.S. Const., art. I, §5, cl. 4). 808472219.S.

[89] Information on recess appointments during recent presidencies may be obtained in the *Weekly Compilation of Presidential Documents*. For President George W. Bush's recess appointments, *see* CRS Report RL33310, *Recess Appointments Made by President George W. Bush*, by Henry B. Hogue and Maureen O. Bearden.

[90] For President Barak Obama's recess appointments, *see* CRS Report R42329, *Recess Appointments Made by President Barack Obama*, by Henry B. Hogue and Maureen O. Bearden.

[91] *Evans*, 387 F.3d at 1226.

[92] *Id.* at 1224-25. ("We do not agree with the Framers' use of the term 'the' unambiguously points to the single recess that comes at the end of a Session. Instead we accept that 'the Recess,' originally and through today, could just as properly refer generically to any one—intrasession or intersession—of the Senate's acts of recessing, that is taking a break." *Id.*).

[93] *Evans*, 387 F.3d at 1225.

[94] *Noel Canning*, 705 F.3d at 506. The distinct facts underlying the January 4, 2012, recess appointments are discussed below. *See infra* "Congressional Scheduling Practice and the January 2012 Recess Appointments."

[95] *Id.* at 500.

[96] *Id.* at 500.

[97] *Id.* at 502 (emphasizing that the Supreme Court in *INS v. Chadha*, 462 U.S. 919 (1983), also considered the increasing frequency of legislative vetoes but ultimately concluded that "the practice of a more recent vintage is less compelling than historical practice dating back to the era of the Framers." *Id.*).

[98] *Id.* at 504. The *Noel Canning* court rejected the vagueness of the Daugherty interpretation, finding that "when interpreting 'major features' of the Constitution's separation of power, we must 'establish[] high walls and clear distinctions because low walls and vague distinctions will not be judicially defensible in the heat of interbranch conflict." *Id.* (*citing* Plaut v. Spendthrift Farm, Inc., 514 U.S. 211(1995)).

[99] *Id.* at 504.

[100] *Id.*

[101] *Id.* at 512-13. According to the court, the first session of the 112th Congress expired simultaneously with the beginning of the second session when the hour of 12 o'clock arrived based on the constitutional limitation. However, the court found that the Senate did not enter "the Recess" between the first and second sessions of the 112th Congress because it declined to adjourn *sine die*. In contrast, the Senate entered "the Recess" between the first and second sessions of the 110th Congress because it adjourned *sine die* after meeting for a *pro forma* session on December 31, 2007. *Id.* at 513.

[102] *Id.* at 514.

[103] *See also* Hogue, *supra* note 3, at 4; Swan v. Clinton, 100 F.3d 973, 987 (D.C. Cir. 1996) (recess appointment is not an "inferior" procedure to appointment with Senate confirmation); Designation of Acting Solicitor Labor, 2002 WL 34461082 (2002) (distinguishing between an temporary designation under the Vacancies Reform Act and a recess appointment—"An acting official does not hold the office, but only 'perform[s] the functions and duties of the office.'[citation omitted] He is not 'appointed' to the office but only 'direct[ed]' or authorized to discharge its functions and duties, and thus he receives the pay of his permanent position, not of the office in which he acts. [citation omitted] A recess appointee, on the other hand, is appointed by one of the methods specified in the Constitution itself, [citation omitted]; he holds the office; and he receives the pay.").

[104] For an exchange on the issue of whether the Senate could alter its recess practices to bring about earlier termination of recess appointments, *see* Seth Barrett Tillman, *Senate Termination of Presidential Recess Appointments*, 101 Nw. U. L. Rev. Colloquy 82 (2007); Brian C. Kalt, *Keeping Recess Appointments in Their Place*, 101 Nw. U. L. Rev. Colloquy 88 (2007); Seth Barrett Tillman, *Terminating Presidential Recess Appointments: A Reply to Professor Brian C. Kalt,* 101 Nw. U. L. Rev. Colloquy 94 (2007); Brian C. Kalt, *Keeping Tillman Adjournments in their Place: A Rejoinder to Seth Barrett Tillman*, 101 Nw. U. L. Rev. Colloquy 108 (2007).

[105] Recess Appointments, 41 Op. Att'y Gen. 463, 470-71 (1960). *See also* 28 Comp. Gen. 121 (1948).

[106] *See* Hogue, *supra* note 3, at 4.

[107] 41 Op. Att'y Gen., *supra* note 105, at 471 (" ... the recess commissions granted during the present recess of the Senate will terminate at the end of the first session of the 87th

Congress. Officers who serve at your pleasure, of course, may be removed by you at any time.").

[108] Term of Office of Major General Patterson as Surgeon General - Recess Appointment, 37 Op. Att'y Gen. 282 (1933). *See also* 9 Comp. Gen. 190 (1929).

[109] *Id.* at 284. The Senate had confirmed and a regular commission was issued to the individual on December 22, 1931.

[110] *Id.* at 284, 287. Other appointments where the individual's term of office related back to the date on which he was recess appointed rather than confirmed include: "A member of the Tariff Commission, 'for a term of twelve years from September 8, 1928, to which office he was appointed during the last recess of the Senate'; a member of the Public Utilities Commission of the District of Columbia, 'for a term of three years from July 1, 1928, to which office he was appointed during the last recess of the Senate,'; a member of the Federal Farm Loan Board, 'for a term of eight years, expiring August 6, 1936 (reappointment)'." *See also* 12 Comp. Gen. 641, 645 (1933).

[111] United States v. Kirkpatrick, 22 U.S. 720, 734 (1824).

[112] *Id.*

[113] 2 Op. Att'y Gen. 333, 335 (1830). *See also* 2 Op. Att'y Gen. 336, 337 (1830); 16 Op. Att'y Gen. 656 (1880) (the Solicitor General, on behalf of the Attorney General, concluded that "[t]he term during which [the Chief Constructor] served under the temporary [recess] appointment was, by law, a different term from that which commenced in April [15,]1878 [the date of the Senate's confirmation]."

[114] *See In re*: Marshalship, 20 Fed. 379 (D. Ala. 1884); Commissions Granted During the Recess of the Senate, 2 Op. Att'y Gen. 336 (1830); 21 Comp. Gen. 789 (1915) (Comptroller of the Treasury). Also, note that a pay restriction may be triggered if the rejected nominee were appointed presumably to a successive recess appointment. It is unclear if this provision affects incumbent recess appointees whose nominations are rejected. The provision would prevent payment to an individual who is in a position "for which he or she has been nominated after the Senate has voted not to approve the nomination of said person." 5 U.S.C. note preceding §5501. *See infra* note 154 and accompanying text.

[115] Power of the President to Fill Vacancies, 2 Op. Att'y Gen. 525 (1832); Power of the President to Fill Vacancies, 3 Op. Att'y Gen. 673 (1841); Power of the President to Appoint to Office During Recess of the Senate, 4 Op. Att'y Gen. 523 (1846); President's Power to Appoint to Office, 11 Op. Att'y Gen. 179 (1865). *See also* 28 Comp. Gen. 30, 38 (1948); 28 Comp. Gen. 121, 129 (1948).

[116] 464 F. Supp. at 601, n.41.

[117] Sharon Block filled a seat that became vacant on January 3, 2012, when the Board member Craig Becker's recess appointment expired. *See* 158 Cong. Rec. S582-83 (daily ed. February 13, 2012).

[118] *Noel Canning*, 705 F.3d at 513.

[119] *See* 3 Op. Off. Legal Counsel, *supra* note 87, at 317 ("A recess appointment presupposes the existence of a vacancy. If there is an incumbent in the office the recess appointment in itself does not effect a removal of the incumbent so as to create a vacancy. Before the President can exercise his recess appointment power in such a case he must exercise his constitutional removal power to the extent it is available, or, if not available, the incumbent must resign" (citations omitted)).

[120] A statutory holdover provision provides for an officer appointed to a fixed term to continue to serve in the office at the expiration of the term for which he or she was appointed. Sometimes this period is opened ended, defined as continuing until a successor is appointed. Other times, this period is limited and continues until either a successor is appointed or a specific period of time has expired.

[121] *See, e.g.*, Appointments to the Board of the Legal Services Corporation, 2005 WL 6086110 (2005); The Inapplicability of the Federal Vacancies Reform Act's Reporting Obligations for PAS Officers Serving Under Statutory Holdover Provisions, 1999 WL 33232455

(1999); Whether Members of the Sentencing Commission Who Were Appointed Prior to the Enactment of a Holdover Statute May Exercise Holdover Rights Pursuant to the Statute, 18 Op. Off. Legal Counsel 123 (1994); Legal Services Corporation—Effect of Statutory Holdover Provisions, 2 Op. Off. Legal Counsel 398 (1978).

[122] Staebler v. Carter, 464 F. Supp. 585 (D.D.C. 1979).

[123] *Id.* at 588 (*citing* FEC statute 2 U.S.C. §437(a)(2) (1976)).

[124] *Id.* at 589. "The plain implication of that language is that a vacancy does indeed occur as a result of and contemporaneously with the expiration of the term of office not some subsequent time." *Id.* at 589-90. Furthermore, the court found that the term "vacancy" was somewhat defined by the statute, which mandates that "a 'vacancy occurring other than by expiration of a term of office' shall be filled only for the remainder of the unexpired term." *Id.*

[125] *Id.* at 597.

[126] *Id.* at 591. *See also* McCalpin v. Dana, No. 82-542 (D.D.C. October 5, 1982) (the President could displace holdover Directors by making recess appointment), *appeal dismissed as moot*, McCalpin v. Durant, 766 F.2d 535 (D.D.C. 1994).

[127] Mackie v. Clinton, 827 F. Supp. 56 (D.D.C. 1993), *vacated as moot*, 10 F.3d 13 (D.C. Cir. 1993).

[128] 39 U.S.C. §202(b).

[129] Mackie, 827 F. Supp. at 58.

[130] *Id.*

[131] 865 F. Supp. 891 (D.D.C. 1994), *rev'd on other grounds*, Wilkinson v. Legal Servs. Corp., 80 F.3d 535 (D.C. Cir. 1996).

[132] *Id.* at 902.

[133] *Id.* at 900-01.

[134] *Id.* at 902.

[135] *See* Hogue, *supra* note 3, *supra*, at 3-4.

[136] *See also* CRS Report RS21412, *Temporarily Filling Presidentially Appointed, Senate-Confirmed Positions*, by Henry B. Hogue.

[137] 5 U.S.C. §§3345-3349d. The Vacancies Act explicitly states that it is the exclusive means for authorizing the temporary filling of advice and consent positions unless otherwise expressly provided in law, or unless the President exercises his authority under the Recess Appointments Clause. The original version of the act was enacted in 1868, 15 Stat. 168 (1868), and its time limitations that limited the duration of a temporary assignee to six months also date back to 1795. 1 Stat 415 (1795).

[138] 12 Stat. 642, 646 (1863). The appropriations rider also provided that no money was to be paid from the Treasury "to any person acting or assuming to act as an officer, civil, military, or naval, as salary in any office, which is not authorized by some previously existing law, unless where such office shall be subsequently sanctioned by law." *Id.*

[139] *See* 33 Cong. Globe 564-65 (1863).

[140] *Id.* at 565.

[141] 14 Stat. 430 (1867).

[142] *Id.*

[143] *Id.* at 431.

[144] *See* Jonathan Turley, *Senate Trials and Factional Disputes: Impeachment as a Madisonian Device*, 40 Duke L.J. 1, 87-88 (1999).

[145] 16 Stat. 6 (1869).

[146] 24 Stat. 500 (1887).

[147] 272 U.S. 52 (1926). The Supreme Court stated: "we have no hesitation in holding that ... the Tenure of Office Act of 1867, in so far as it attempted to prevent the President from removing executive officers who had been appointed by him by and with the advice and consent of the Senate, was invalid, and that subsequent legislation of the same effect was equally so." *Id.* at 176. *But see* Humphrey's Executor v. United States, 295 U.S. 602, 627

(1935) (upholding a statutory restriction on the President's ability to remove the head of an independent agency and distinguishing its holding from *Meyers* by stating that *Myers* was limited to "purely executive officers").

[148] It had been previously codified as Rev. Stat. §1761 ch.580, 54 Stat. 751 (1940).

[149] This pay restriction to recess appointees applies to those positions that receive pay from the Treasury of the United States. *See, e.g.*, Permissibility of Recess Appointments of Directors of the Federal Housing Finance Board, 15 Op. Off. Legal Counsel 91, 93 (1991) (concluding that because none of the payment for the Directors came from the Treasury that the pay restriction of 5 U.S.C. §5503 did not apply to the recess appointees).

[150] *See* 15 Op. Off. Legal Counsel, *supra* note 149, at 93 ("Although its language is far from clear, section 5503(a) has been interpreted as prohibiting the payment of compensation to successive recess appointees.").

[151] Recess Appointments Issues, 6 Op. Off. Legal Counsel 585, 586 (1982) (emphasis added); Recess Appointments, 41 Op. Att'y Gen. 463, 472-73 n.13 (1960) (citing 52 Comp. Gen. 556, 557 (1973); 36 Comp. Gen. 444 (1956)).

[152] *See* 28 Comp. Gen. 238, 240-41 (1948) ("The use of the general or indefinite term 'a,' as opposed to the specific or definite article 'the,' reasonably may be regarded as contemplating that the requirements of the [subsection (a)(2)] are satisfied if any nomination for the office is pending before the Senate for its consideration, rather than the nomination of the particular individual who receives the recess appointment. ... [I]t would seem that the right [to be paid] is unaffected by the fact that the one subsequently given the recess appointment is not the same person whose nomination was submitted to the Senate.").

[153] Oftentimes the same individual is both the nominee and the recess appointee. If such is the case, then it seems clear that such an individual who is recess appointed a second time would not be paid under §5503(a)(2). However, if individual A was the recess appointee and had a pending nomination to the position and then individual B is later recess appointed upon the expiration of individual A's commission, then based on Department of Justice and Comptroller General interpretations, it seems possible that individual B could be paid under §5503(a)(2). Alternatively, if individual A continues to be the nominee while individual B is given a first and second recess appointment, an argument could forwarded that individual B could be paid under the express terms of §5503(a)(2).

[154] 5 U.S.C. note preceding §5501; P.L. 110-161, 121 Stat. 2021 (2007) ("Hereafter, no part of any appropriation contained in this or any other Act shall be paid to any person for the filling of any position for which he or she has been nominated after the Senate has voted not to approve the nomination of said person."); *See, e.g.*, P.L. 108-447, Div. H, §609; 118 Stat. 3274. It is also worth noting that for FY2009, Congress enacted another permanent appropriations rider that would prohibit payment "to any individual carrying out the responsibilities of any position requiring Senate advice and consent in an acting or temporary capacity after the second submission of a nomination for that individual to that position has been withdrawn or returned to the President." P.L. 111-8; 123 Stat. 693 (2009). Though this provision seems designed to prevent payment to persons appointed in accordance with the Vacancies Reform Act, a question may arise as to whether this prohibition could extend to recess appointees, given that they are arguably acting in a "temporary capacity."

[155] H.Rept. 76-2646 (76th Cong., 3d sess. 1940).

[156] *Id.*

[157] 28 Comp. Gen. 30, 37 (1948); *see also* 41 Op. Att'y Gen, *supra n*ote 105, at 473-75.

[158] *See* Trish Turner, "Democrats Fight Sam Fox Nomination, Charge He Cannot Serve Without Pay," Fox News Corp., April 5, 2007, *available at* http://www.foxnews.com/story/0,2933,264420,00.html.

[159] 31 U.S.C. §1342.

[160] The prohibition codified 31 U.S.C. §1342 was enacted in response to a practice common late in the 19th century under which lower grade government employees were asked to "volunteer" their services for overtime work and agencies subsequently requested additional appropriations from Congress to pay them. Government Accountability Office (GAO), Office of the General Counsel, *II Principles of Federal Appropriations Law*, 6-95, 3d Ed. (February 2006).

[161] *Id.* at 95-96.

[162] *Id.* at 102.

[163] The GAO has relied upon this dynamic in determining that the voluntary services prohibition does not preclude the service of a recess appointee falling within the pay proscriptions codified at 5 U.S.C. §5503, even in instances where the compensation of the position in question is fixed by statute. Addressing the recess appointment of Sam Fox to serve as Ambassador to Belgium under circumstances triggering a §5503 payment prohibition, the GAO noted that while the rate of compensation for such a position is set by statute, "[t]he Department of State may allow him to serve without compensation, despite the voluntary services prohibition of the Antideficiency Act, because Mr. Fox's service would not result in a coercive deficiency or a subsequent claim against the Government, which was the original justification behind the prohibition. Mr. Fox could not make such a claim because of the statutory bar of section 5503." GAO, *Recess Appointment of Sam Fox*, B-309301 at 7-8 (June 8, 2007). The GAO further stated that "an alternative interpretation that would directly curtail the President's power to make a recess appointment to Mr. Fox would raise serious constitutional concerns." *Id.* at 8.

[164] *Staebler*, 464 F. Supp. at 596 n.24.

[165] *See* Halstead, *supra* note 55, at 11.

[166] *See, e.g.*, Constitutional Law-Article II, Section 2, Clause 3- Recess Appointments-Compensation (5 U.S.C. §5503), 3 Op. Off. Legal Counsel 314 (1979); Reimbursement of Expenses Under 5 U.S.C. §5503(a), 22 Op. Off. Legal Counsel 29 (1998).

[167] *Evans*, 387 F.3d at 1235. Note that in denying the petition for *writ of certiorari*, Justice Stevens commented that "it would be a mistake to assume that our disposition of this petition constitutes a decision on the merits of whether the President has the constitutional authority to fill future Article III vacancies, such as vacancies on this Court, with appointments made absent consent of the Senate during short intrasession 'recesses.'" Evans v. Stephens, 544 U.S. 942, 943 (2004) (order denying petition for *writ of certiorari*).

[168] *Noel Canning*, 705 F.3d at 506.

[169] *See supra* notes 76 and 83 and accompany text.

[170] Glossary, http://www.senate.gov.

[171] 153 Cong. Rec. S14609 (daily ed. November 16, 2007) (Senator Harry Reid, "Recess Appointments," remarks in the Senate). Though this statement specifically indicates the use of *pro forma* sessions to prevent recess appointments, Senator Reid on at least one other occasion indicated that the Senate would be holding *pro forma* sessions for different purposes. On September 17, 2008, he stated, "We are going to have to get some committee hearings underway, which is why we are not going to adjourn. We will be in pro forma session so committees can still meet, though we won't have any activities here on the floor as relates to these markets." 154 Cong. Rec. S8907 (daily ed. September 17, 2008) (Senator Harry Reid, "The Economy," remarks in the Senate).

[172] *See* Hogue, *supra* note 3, at 2-3.

[173] *See* Haynes, *supra* note 33, at 772-73.

[174] 106 Cong. Rec. 18145 (1960).

[175] The resolution provided that it was the sense of the Senate that this type of recess appointment "is not wholly consistent with the best interests of the Supreme Court, the nominee who may be involved, the litigants before the Court, nor indeed the people of the United States." The resolution further announced the position that such appointments should be avoided "except under unusual and urgent circumstances." 106 Cong. Rec. 12761 (1960).

[176] U.S. Congress, Senate, Senator David Vitter, "Vitter, DeMint Urge House to Block Controversial Recess Appointments," press release (May 25, 2011). Similarly, many House Representatives requested to the Speaker of the House and other majority leaders that "all appropriate measures be taken to prevent any and all recess appointments by preventing the Senate from officially recessing for the remainder of the 112th Congress." U.S. Congress, House, Representative Jeff Landry, Letter to the Speaker of the House John Boehner, et al., (Jun, 15, 2011).

[177] U.S. Const., amend. XX, §2.

[178] 157 Cong. Rec. S8783 (daily digest December 17, 2011); 153 Cong. Rec. S14609 (daily ed. November 16, 2007).

[179] *See* White House, press release, January 4, 2012, *available at* http://www.whitehouse.gov/the-press-office/2012/01/04/president-obama-announces-recess-appointments-key-administra tion-posts; and White House Blog, America's Consumer Watchdog, January 4, 2012, *available at* http://www.whitehouse.gov/blog/2012/01/04/americas-consumer- watchdog.

[180] *See, e.g.*, Alan K. Ota, *Senate Republicans Consider Responses to Obama's Recess Appointments*, CQ Online (January 4, 2012); and Lauren Smith, *Recess Appointments to NLRB Draw GOP Criticism*, CQ Online, (January 4, 2012). *See* Lyle Denniston, *Spreading challenge to appointment power (UPDATED)*, SCOTUSblog, January 28, 2013, *available at* http://www.scotusblog.com/2013/01/spreading-challenge-to-appointment-power/; *Complaint, State Nat'l Bank of Big Spring v. Geithner, Case No. 1.12-cv-01032 (D.C. September 20, 2012), available at* http://newsandinsight.thomsonreuters.com/ uploaded Files/Reuters_Content/2012/09_-_September/statenationvcfpb--amendedcomplaint.pdf; Opposition to Receiver's Second Request for Payment, Consumer Fin. Prot. Bureau v. Gordon, Case No. CV12-6147-RSWL(MRWx), (C.D.Cal. July 18, 2012), *available at* http://www.cfpbmonitor.com/files/2013/ 02/CGCFPB-Opp-Rec-Req-2.pdf.

[181] *Noel Canning*, 705 F.3d at 514. The court narrowly interpreted the two key phrases of the Clause—"the Recess" and "Vacanc[y] that may happen"—stating that "the Recess" is limited to intersession recesses where the Senate has adjourned *sine die*, and that only a vacancy that arises during "the Recess" may be filled during that intersession recess. *Id.*

[182] *See supra* note 8.

[183] Nat'l Labor Relations Bd. v. Noel Canning, No. 12-1281, 2013 U.S. LEXIS 4876 (Jun. 24, 2013).

[184] U.S. Const., art. I, §5, cl. 4. *See* DOJ brief, *supra* note 83, and accompanying text. Similarly, a court may explore whether there also needs to be a requisite number of days for an intersession recess to occur, or may the constitutional end of one session and the beginning of another session be treated as a "constructive" recess?

[185] Lawfulness of Recess Appointments During a Recess of the Senate Notwithstanding Periodic Pro Forma Sessions, 2012 WL 168645 (January 6, 2012) (*citing* 33 Op. Att'y Gen., *supra* note 73, at 25).

INDEX

D

E

F

T

U

V

W